"A powerful and practical guide for leaders who want to build a career on a foundation of trust and ethical action. *The Integrity Edge* isn't just about doing the right thing; it's about unlocking true competitive advantage."

— **Mohammad Anwar,** CEO of Softway & Culture+, coauthor of the *Wall Street Journal* bestseller *Love as a Business Strategy* and *Love as a Change Strategy*

"When asked what one thing I would tell people about achieving success, I have always said that it's all relationships, and that the foundation of relationships is trust. In *The Integrity Edge*, Rusty Atkinson gets to the heart of relationships, trust, and more. This is a book I would advise business leaders to buy for themselves and every member of their team. Then talk about it. Get aligned with the principles in *The Integrity Edge*, and your success, in business and in life, is assured."

— **Joe Calloway**, author of *Be the Best at What Matters Most*

"In *The Integrity Edge*, Rusty distills thirty years of leadership experience into practical frameworks and authentic storytelling. With refreshing transparency, he shares both his triumphs and setbacks—offering invaluable lessons on aligning personal values with professional ambition. The result is a compelling guide for anyone navigating the path of purposeful leadership."

— **Dave Wagner**, president and CEO, Everbridge

"Every leader should read this book. *The Integrity Edge* exposes the high cost of compromised leadership and offers a daring alternative: rise with integrity, lead with courage, and win the right way."

— **Frank Danna**, *Wall Street Journal* bestselling author and cofounder at Culture+

"Whether you're a first-time manager or a seasoned executive, *The Integrity Edge* will help you become a better leader at work (and life). This is an engaging, useful, and practical book. Rusty doesn't hold back. He shares generously. *The Integrity Edge* is not the kind of book you read and let it collect dust. This is a leadership book that will serve you in all seasons of your journey."

— **Ali Merchant**, founder of All-In Manager, former head of L&D

"Nothing destroys teams or organizations more quickly than leaders who lack integrity, but how one develops integrity can feel mysterious. Rusty Atkinson not only reveals the stumbling blocks that trip leaders up but also practical ways that leaders can intentionally grow their character. *The Integrity Edge* should be required reading for every current and aspiring leader."

—**Dr. Garland Vance**, co-founder of AdVance Leadership

THE
INTEGRITY
EDGE

UNLOCKING THE HIDDEN POWER OF
ETHICAL LEADERSHIP

RUSTY ATKINSON

First Edition: 2025

ISBN: 979-8-9997953-0-4 (Paperback)
ISBN: 979-8-9997953-1-1 (Hardback)
ISBN: 979-8-9997953-2-8 (ebook)

For information about permissions, bulk purchases,
or speaking engagements, please contact:

Rusty Atkinson
rusty@rustyatkinson.com

Edited by Janelle DeBlaay
Text design and composition by John Reinhardt Book Design

DISCLAIMER: The information presented in this book is intended for general educational purposes. The author and publisher make no guarantees regarding the outcome of applying the principles described herein, and they shall not be held liable for any loss or damages resulting from the use of this material.

NOTE ON ANONYMITY: To protect the privacy of individuals and organizations, some names, dates, roles, and identifying details have been changed. In some cases, details or elements have been intentionally fabricated or blended to further obscure identities. While the core events and leadership lessons remain true, composite characters or scenarios may have been used to preserve confidentiality without compromising the message.

Printed in the United States of America

To Paulette, Lauren, and Chase.
But for the grace of God and the love of my family.

CONTENTS

INTRODUCTION
Debunking the Leadership Lie

"The time is always right to do what is right."
—MARTIN LUTHER KING JR.[i]

E ARLY IN MY CAREER, I had a front-row seat to a situation that is emblematic of a specific dysfunction in corporate leadership—a dysfunction that seems everpresent.

It was in the mid-2000s and I was working as an IT director for a large, US-based technology company. I worked for weeks to define a solution to our company's long-standing technical problem. It was the sort of problem that one or two actions wouldn't solve. This was a complex, systemic problem that required the attention of the entire technology organization to resolve. Over the course of a couple of weeks, I put together an action plan—highly detailed in parts and superficially detailed in other parts. I knew I needed my peers' time, attention, and experience to develop and execute this plan. I had done what I could with the resolution and needed help.

I reached out to my direct manager. He was a man I knew I could trust, with whom I had a great relationship. I pitched the problem statement and my solution to my manager. We had a spirited discussion about the plan—what he liked, what he thought was missing, what he thought would work well, and where he thought we might struggle. After several such discussions, my plan—now our plan—was in better shape. We agreed it was time for me to pitch our plan to his boss. His boss was a technology executive we believed had sufficient authority and influence to give this plan a chance to succeed.

We scheduled the presentation with this technology executive. The meeting would include just me, my boss, and my boss's boss. I would pitch the problem and solution, we would get the executive's thoughts, and determine the next steps.

The presentation went well. I thought I made the problem clear, and succinctly stated the approach we were advocating. But the presentation fell flat. The executive barely engaged. He asked a few shallow questions and thanked me for the effort, but dismissed the plan as impractical. He said something like, "We have more important priorities than this right now."

I was disappointed. I had worked so hard. I was excited about the plan. I knew it could help resolve a long-standing problem that impacted nearly every one of this executive's teams. Nevertheless, I had been working for large technology organizations long enough to know there were far more things going on in a company, and far more forces influencing our priorities, than I was aware of. If the boss said it wasn't the right time, I was sure he was correct.

I remember thinking I was happy I got to develop the plan and present it to the executive. As an ambitious technology leader, I knew I needed experience developing, presenting, and championing this sort of large-scale initiative, and that was the silver lining in this attempt. Plus, I could enact the parts of the strategy that were in my area of responsibility. They would add value, though far less than I had imagined in my planning; I could pursue those parts without requiring additional funding or personnel. I had all the authority I needed to execute part of the plan. Despite not getting the support I hoped for, I thought it was a beneficial endeavor.

The following week, perhaps three or four days after my presentation, the executive I presented to called his organization's managers to an urgent meeting. This would be a meeting of twenty or so managers, senior managers, directors, and senior directors. Details were sparse, but the topic was important.

Since ours was a geographically dispersed team with leaders across much of the United States and India, all the managers joined a teleconference. This was well before the widespread use of video in large meetings. The executive joined and, with little preamble, he launched into his talk. He told us he had been struggling with a specific issue that plagued his team. He said he had been wrestling with the best way to solve this issue for months. Then, while struggling to fall asleep the previous weekend, he had an epiphany. It was an epiphany so exciting and with such potential that he got up in the middle of the night to work on the details. He didn't want to fall asleep and lose momentum.

With that as a backdrop, he proceeded to share the plan I had pitched to him just days earlier.

My manager was on instant messenger with me immediately. He urged me to be calm. He told me it was clear the executive was trying to pass my plan off as his personal epiphany. He all but begged me to take a deep breath before I said or did anything I might regret. No, my manager did not know this was going to happen. No, my manager was not involved in the coverup. No, my manager couldn't believe this was happening. Like me, he was in shock.

The executive even used the same title for the complex initiative. His epiphany had the same exact title as the plan I presented to him. In a few short days, my plan went from impractical, something the executive could not see prioritizing, to being the cornerstone of this leader's departmental strategy. And all without so much as a mention of my involvement. The executive said he woke up in the middle of the night with this idea and worked all weekend on the details.

Over the following days, my manager and I discussed my possible response. Ultimately, I decided not to confront the executive with his deceit. I knew how impactful the plan could be and how much the organization needed to boost productivity. I theorized that if I pressed this issue, the strategy would lose the executive's support, and my position—and my manager's position—could be negatively impacted. I could let the deception stand and reap the benefit of the subsequent improvements, or I could challenge him, continue to struggle with the root problem, and potentially paint a target on our backs in the process. As much as it disgusted me, I wanted the plan to succeed and transform our team more than I wanted credit.

As I said, this episode is emblematic of a specific dysfunction I have witnessed time after time in the corporate world: senior leaders who act in self-serving ways and make decisions focused on personal gain and impact over how they affect the company or the people on their team.

In my experience, ethical action and integrity seem to be more common in junior leaders. It is as if something happens between the junior and senior ranks that blocks people of good character from getting promoted. Or, is it possible that a leader is forced to sacrifice their integrity and embrace a self-serving, egocentric leadership style to get promoted? Perhaps all leaders start out as ethical leaders but change in order to reach the next rung on the ladder.

Throughout my career, I have seen evidence suggesting that if you desire to grow your career as an organizational leader, you must be willing—even adept—at treating the people in your charge as tools whose sole purpose is pursuing your personal agenda. Their career growth, job satisfaction, and personal happiness are insignificant, even irrelevant. How can they serve you and your aspirations? Nothing else matters if you want to be successful in the corporate world.

How can that be? How can "doing the right thing" and treating people fairly create a career ceiling? How can being a person of character be a handicap to career growth?

I have learned it does not have to be this way. Leadership models focusing on "doing the right thing" for employees can lead to a successful career. Leadership models focusing on service, trust, and honesty can lead the practitioner to the C-suite. I have seen many ethical leaders in senior and executive roles. I have held many vice-president and senior vice-president roles, and have been a member of the C-Suite at two separate companies while being a practitioner and vocal advocate for ethical, service-oriented leadership. I have established inclusive, compassionate servant leadership as a core pillar of my personal identity, and have been able to grow my career to the C-suite. I believe I reached the C-suite in large part because I tightly linked my personal identity to an ethical, inclusive, service-oriented approach to leadership. I have witnessed firsthand the distinct advantages my approach has over the more commonly trodden path. This is what I refer to as the "integrity edge."

Leadership models focusing on "doing the right thing" for employees can lead to a successful career.

ENDS AND MEANS

Does it matter? As long as I advance, does it matter how I go about advancing? Don't the ends justify the means? Why risk it?

It matters for three reasons:

1. The ends do not justify the means. How we do something is important.
2. Valuing the ends over the means is a path to compromise and unethical actions.
3. The integrity edge is a competitive differentiator.

Ultimately, it comes down to what you prioritize. If your priority is advancement at any cost, this book is not for you. I understand some people hold this point of view. This book does not address that strategy.

But if you determine that your priority is to advance "the right way," if you decide that your advancement is important, but you want to treat people well in the process, act in a trustworthy manner, and generally not be a jerk as you advance in your leadership responsibilities, this book is definitely for you.

Are you still here? That must mean you have decided advancing in "the right way" is preferable to advancing "at any cost." That is great! It is possible to advance your leadership career ethically, but it will not happen automatically. The path of ethical advancement is simple, but it will not always be easy.

INTRODUCING THE INTEGRITY EDGE

In the next chapter I'll unpack the integrity edge in more detail, but first, let me just say the integrity edge refers to the competitive advantage experienced in environments where demonstrated integrity results in trust and respect. This advantage manifests in superior culture and employee engagement. Leading with integrity fosters an environment where employees feel safe and supported to take risks, innovate, and strive for stretch goals. Ultimately, the integrity edge is a term that captures the net impact of high-integrity leadership on an organization's teams, culture, and outcomes.

Let's arm ourselves with a simple strategy for ethical advancement that results in a strategic advantage:

1. Commit to the ethical approach now.
2. Recognize the risks to ethical advancement and understand why these risks commonly occur.
3. Equip yourself with specific plans to avoid these risks as your career advances.

It really is that simple. Ethical advancement relies on a commitment to doing the right thing, and being prepared for the forces that will attempt to derail your advancement.

THE LEADERSHIP CHOICE
THAT DEFINES YOU

An old Chinese proverb states, "The best time to plant a tree was twenty years ago. The second-best time is now." The best time to commit to being an ethical leader, humbly focused on serving the team you are leading, is before your first leadership role begins. The second-best time to commit to this approach is now.

Ideally, you are reading this book in preparation for a career in leading others. Perhaps you are entering the workforce and have been struggling to rationalize the actions of successful leaders with your personal morals. Perhaps you are concerned that you cannot be the person you want to be and have a successful leadership career at the same time, so you have picked up this book in hopes you will discover a path that allows you to advance ethically. If that is you, welcome.

Some readers will find this book well after their leadership career is underway. You have seen the challenges that arise and some of the costs of practicing ethical leadership firsthand. Some leaders have done well, advancing their careers without compromising their principles. Some have done okay, perhaps with a few missteps along the way. Others have started chasing their career goals with an "at any cost" approach, but also find themselves hoping there is a better way. I want to welcome you as well.

It does not matter where you are in your career—beginning, middle, or near the end—you can decide to start leading ethically today. You can start changing how you respond to leadership challenges now, and start leading the way you aspire to.

But it starts with commitment. It starts with a decision to seek and find the ethical path to leadership advancement and to follow that path. Making this commitment is the key.

How many of you have wanted to start a new behavior? You want to start exercising more. You want to change your diet. You want to drink less. You want to read more. You want to get more sleep. Each of these behaviors is easy to perform once but hard to do consistently. Going to the gym instead of bingeing a program on TV is easy to do one time but hard to do four times a week. Ugh. However, once you commit to being the person who goes to the gym and begin identifying with that lifestyle, the decision is easier.

My wife and I have been married for over thirty years. Very early in our marriage we both worked in jobs that required us to travel from time to time. Typical of business travel, we would be on the road for several days a week, staying at hotels with coworkers, eating and spending time together. It didn't take long for each of us to witness our colleagues drinking too much and making terrible, life-impacting choices. We saw firsthand, after a night of drinking, individuals who claim to be happily married walking off to their hotel rooms with people who were not their spouses. It happened with heartbreaking frequency.

At the time, my wife and I both occasionally enjoyed having a few drinks and unwinding. It was a normal part of our socializing. But as much as we enjoyed socializing in this way, we enjoyed our new marriage more. We discussed what we both witnessed while traveling and devised a plan. We committed to one another that we would not consume alcohol unless we were together.

This commitment has served us well. Sure, initially it was tough. The colleagues we had been traveling with for months noticed when we didn't buy a drink. We brushed it off and said something like, "I just don't feel like drinking tonight." But when one night became every night, our friends pressed, and we revealed the reason for our decision. Even now, when we share that we only drink when we are together, some people truly do not understand. But for me and Paulette, it makes all the sense in the world.

Now, after more than thirty years, we are not the young, work-all-day-and-stay-up-all-night types we were when we made this commitment. But our commitment has not changed, and a fascinating thing has happened after all these years. Being the guy who only consumes alcohol when he is with his wife has become part of my identity. People who have known me for years know this about me and no longer question it. It has become part of my identity to me, as well. Now, when I have to answer the question "Why aren't you having a drink?" for a new acquaintance, it is much easier to tell my story. At this point, it would feel like being unfaithful to my wife if I had a drink when she was not with me. It has become easy to keep the commitment I made thirty years ago.

A similar thing will happen when you commit to being an ethical leader. This commitment will differentiate you from your peers. At first, it will just be seen as something you do. But eventually, it will become who you are. You will establish a reputation for service, humility, and inclusion. People will expect you to act in a certain way, to treat people in a certain way, and to respond in a certain way. When you make the commitment and act in ways that align with that commitment, you will establish an identity as an ethical leader. That identity will make each ethical decision easier than the last. When what makes you different becomes your identity, companies, leaders, and employees who desire those traits will hold you in higher regard. Your commitment to ethical advancement will become part of your value proposition and will actually help with your career advancement. It will manifest the integrity edge.

SOONER IS EASIER

Ideally, leaders commit to ethical advancement early in their careers. While it is possible to change your leadership approach well into your career, the change becomes more difficult as the years go by. Your responsibilities grow in scope and scale, and the ramifications of your decisions increase. Establishing your identity as an ethical leader early in your career will make your decisions easier later on.

It's like the life of an athlete. Regardless of the sport or the level of competition they achieve, every athlete started their career with a single game. In that first game, the athlete was not a superstar—they were likely a clumsy, stumbling mess that barely understood the rules, to say nothing of proper technique. For many of these players, the first game held no consequences or rewards outside of having fun. The goal at that time was to introduce concepts, gauge interest, and have fun.

As time passes, the athlete shows interest in the sport, and the coaching changes. The coaching gets more specific and more intense. The training grows in complexity. The games begin to have bigger rewards and consequences.

The athlete learned to play the game when the stakes were low, when the impact of mistakes was virtually non-existent. Throughout their career, the stakes increased, and the impact of missteps increased. At the end of their career, any mistake could cause defeat, and losses could have a monumental impact in terms of finances, fame, and legacy. If the athlete waited until the Olympics to learn proper technique, what are the chances of their success? Proper technique was introduced in the first game and improved and reinforced at every level of their career growth.

This is how ethical leadership principles and actions are learned—over time, with practice, and before the stakes are Olympic.

As individual contributors, we are introduced to dilemmas and conflict. We begin to see instances when we can make the easy choice or the right choice. The impact and consequences at this stage are typically limited to ourselves.

When we become a manager, our decisions impact a few individuals to an extent—who has to work on Saturday, who gets a great performance review, whose evaluation demands an improvement plan. As a director, the number of lives we impact increases, and the intensity of impact increases—layoffs, pay raises, promotions, and hiring decisions. The pattern continues until, as an executive, the scope of influence is complete—all employees and aspects of work life are in your purview.

This is how ethical leadership principles and actions are learned—over time, with practice, and before the stakes are Olympic.

The decisions we make as executives are informed by the habits, behaviors, and decisions we make as vice presidents, directors, managers, and individual contributors. By the time we are executives, we have faced many ethical decisions and have made many choices. Each time the choices we make are ethical, the easier it gets to make the next ethical decision. We develop a sort of ethical muscle memory. We gain experience navigating the waters of corporate decision-making and know where some of the pitfalls lie. We learned to make good decisions when the stakes and consequences were manager-level, and reinforced our patterns as directors and vice presidents. We would be ill-equipped to continue to make good choices if we waited until we were executives to start acting with humility or serving our team members. Actually, we would fail if we waited until we were executives to start acting ethically.

Start now, when the stakes and consequences are comparatively less, and you will be best prepared when the stakes and consequences are magnified.

STUMBLING BLOCKS

Wouldn't it be helpful if you could buy a road map for life? What if you could go to Amazon and browse a selection of situation-specific advisories for the things that are most likely to trip you up? When you plan on asking that special person to marry you, you buy the "Marriage Stumbling Blocks" road map. Amazon would send you an illustrative list of the things you will run into and how you can best avoid the typical tripping hazards. How great would that be?

In this book, I outline the most common stumbling blocks to advancing your leadership career with integrity. They say one ounce of prevention is worth a pound of cure. Because we are identifying the likely stumbling blocks and devising effective strategies to deal with them beforehand, we will be better prepared to deal with tough situations when they occur. And occur they will.

We will examine six common stumbling blocks and explain why they are detrimental to pursuing ethical advancement as a humble, service-minded leader. But I won't just leave you with a list of the most common causes of the death of ethical leadership failure. I will also arm you with effective strategies for avoiding each stumbling block so you can flip the script, turning the potential derailer into a differentiator characterized by integrity and service.

Lack of Trust

Trust is the cornerstone of leadership. Most ethical leadership relies on a foundation of mutual trust between the leader and the team members. Senior leaders experience the lack-of-trust stumbling block when they begin to devalue the importance of cultivating and encouraging trust within their organization. Trust is fragile. If it is not purposefully

The Six Stumbling Blocks

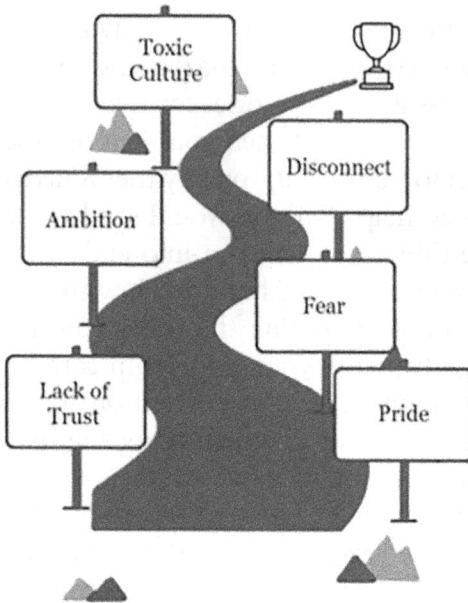

developed and nurtured, it will die. Once trust in an organization dies, it is difficult to regrow. Without trust, a leader will often believe their teams will only respond to a dictator-like approach.

Pride

Leaders change as they accomplish more and grow in their abilities. They begin believing they deserve to be treated differently. They start to think less about how they can help the individuals on their team and more about how important they are to the company or mission. Their leadership becomes less about the team members and more about finding ways to showcase their greatness. The pride stumbling block causes many leaders to stray from the path of ethical advancement.

Fear

Fear is a powerful motivator. The fear stumbling block causes leaders to second-guess their motives and actions. They begin to bypass their service-based leadership actions in favor of "less risky" actions. Having accomplished and achieved so much, they begin to fear it could all be taken away—compensation, power, and prestige. These fears are real and have caused more than one leader to move into protective mode and change their leadership approach.

Ambition

As some leaders move into increasingly senior roles, they start to focus more on short-term outcomes and satisfying critical stakeholders' expectations. More than one leader has made destructive decisions to "make the quarter." More than one leader has agreed to an end-of-fiscal-year layoff to satisfy board expectations. In these cases, the leader may feel they have no other choice, and perhaps in some cases that is true. The ambition stumbling block is not about making difficult, thankless decisions that impact the lives of your employees. This stumbling block is apparent when leaders stop considering the impact these short-term and stakeholder-driven decisions have on their team members. The ambition stumbling block happens when leaders make decisions based solely on how those choices help them advance their objectives, aspirations, and careers. As the leader, you have signed up to make difficult decisions. However, you have stumbled on your own ambition when you stop championing your team and advocating for their well-being in favor of keeping your board or boss happy and advancing your career.

Disconnect

Leadership is a relationship sport. Service-minded leaders are focused on identifying and removing encumbrances from their team members. This type of leader is asking questions, listening to the answers, and finding solutions to the problems their team members are facing. Employees can be reluctant about being transparent with their leaders, believing any admission of the challenges they are facing could cause doubt in their abilities. To overcome this reluctance, the service-minded leader must establish relationships and connections with their team members. Losing touch with the team and devaluing these relationships is where the disconnect stumbling block occurs. Leaders who trip on this block stop asking questions, or when they do ask questions, they stop listening and acting on what they hear. Gradually, the team members stop answering, speaking up, or expecting the leader to help in times of struggle.

Toxic Culture

Company and team culture are not words on a poster. Culture is the evidence of shared values and actions that shape a company or team. Culture can be a powerful, positive force that service-minded leaders can tap into to support their ethical advancement. Cultures that value service, collaboration, and trustworthiness can be a tailwind to your ethical advancement. Culture becomes a stumbling block when the culture of the company or team is in opposition to humble, service-minded leadership. Toxic, compromising company culture can elevate outcomes above all else, prioritize growth and power, and reward selfish ambition over service. When you find yourself in this type of toxic culture, you can be drawn away from your commitment to leading with integrity, often without initially realizing it.

While not an exhaustive list, lack of trust, pride, fear, ambition, disconnect, and toxic culture are common stumbling blocks that cause well-meaning, service-focused leaders to make compromising decisions every day.

What can we do as leaders to protect ourselves from taking shortcuts? What habits and processes can leaders who are just beginning their careers cultivate to guard themselves against the tendencies that seem to plague many leaders as they advance in their fields?

These are the questions we will answer in the following chapters. We will examine each of these stumbling blocks, explore how and why they can distract you from your commitment to service-minded leadership and ethical advancement, and arm you with specific strategies that will help you avoid these stumbling blocks and diminish their impact on your leadership journey.

THE INTEGRITY EDGE
What It Is and Why It Matters

*"What you do speaks so loudly
that I cannot hear what you say."*

—RALPH WALDO EMERSON[ii]

'VE HAD THE PRIVILEGE of working with Doug three times over the years—once as a peer and twice when he joined my team. The first time I hired him, we built something strong together. We worked hard, built a great team, and delivered outstanding results for several years. But changes happen in the corporate world. A corporate restructuring forced me to make one of the hardest decisions a leader ever faces: I had to let him go.

That kind of moment stays with you. Not because of the layoff itself—we've both been around long enough to understand the business realities—but because of what it meant. Doug understood the realities of corporate responsibility and stewardship. He was disappointed, but he told me he understood. The real pain of the moment emanated from the fear I had about what this would do to our relationship. Trust feels fragile when you have to make a decision that hurts someone you care about. I worried I might never get the chance to work with Doug again. After all, who would come back to work with someone who already "fired" you once?

But a few years later, I found myself in a new role and a new opportunity opened up. It was perfect for Doug. I waffled for a bit, wondering if Doug would even consider working with me again. Ultimately, I picked up the phone. Doug answered the call and listened to my pitch. He didn't hesitate. He said yes.

Doug told me something I've carried with me ever since. He said, "I'll always want to work with you because of the shadow of a leader."

Doug talks a lot about the "shadow of a leader." It is a term coined by Larry Senn and Jim Hart in their 1994 book, *21st Century Leadership: Dialogues with 100 Top Leaders.* "Shadow of a leader" refers to the powerful, often unspoken influence a leader has on the culture, behavior, and values of their team or organization. It's the idea that people tend to mirror the actions, priorities, and attitudes of their leaders—whether positive or negative.

He explained he wasn't just following a job. He was following a leader. "I know what kind of organization I'm walking into," he said, "because I know what kind of man I'll be working for. I trust you. That is hard to find and worth following." [iii]

Doug reminds me that trust doesn't start with words—it starts with actions. Integrity has a ripple effect and leadership isn't just about strategy—it's about being someone worth following.

Larry Senn and Jim Hart told us that a leader's actions—good and bad—influence the culture and behavior of their teams. The positive, uplifting impact of ethical leadership is what I call the integrity edge.

The integrity edge is the sustainable, competitive advantage leaders gain when they consistently choose to lead with character, prioritizing trust and service even when it's hard. It is the real and measurable benefit that comes from prioritizing people over ego, trust over fear, and long-term impact over short-term wins. Leaders who prioritize leading well and caring for their teams not only achieve success, but create teams, cultures, and organizations where people thrive and where leadership becomes easier, not harder, over time.

The integrity edge manifests in two primary ways: personal advantages to the leader and distinct benefits to the organization and team.

THE PERSONAL EDGE

When leaders commit to the integrity edge, they are not just making life better for their teams—they are transforming their own leadership experience. The benefits to the leader are profound, personal, and lasting. These benefits are not abstract ideals; they are tangible, everyday advantages that reshape how a leader thinks, decides, and relates.

Many leaders live with a quiet, nagging conflict—the tension between what they know is right and what they do to survive politically. They often make convenient decisions that do not agree with their values. Ethical leaders sidestep this conflict entirely. Ethical leadership brings who you are and how you lead into alignment.

When your actions match your values, your leadership becomes less burdensome and more fulfilling. Decisions become clearer because they are anchored in a moral framework. You are free from the stress of managing contradictions or covering up decisions you regret. You sleep better. Literally. Integrity gives you peace of mind. Life brings enough stress; the integrity edge is, among other things, a cheat code to reduce stress.

Integrity-based leaders can be confident because their decisions are rooted in principles, not politics. They tend to be freed from second-guessing because their choices align with their core beliefs. They can be unburdened by the fear of being "found out" since they have nothing to hide. Authenticity builds self-respect and, in turn, earns the respect of others.

Integrity accelerates trust. Ethical leaders build deep, trust-based relationships with peers, employees, and even their bosses. They attract others who value honesty, consistency, and transparency. These leaders inspire loyalty—not because of position or power, but because of character.

Though some might believe integrity slows a person's career, the opposite can be true. Ethical leadership is a differentiator. Integrity-based leaders stand out in environments desperate for people who are trustworthy and competent. Their reputation may open doors others can't access. They are sought after by organizations that value sustainable, healthy cultures.

Not all organizations value honesty, service, and integrity, but many do. Savvy senior leaders in such organizations seek out leaders who will add to the positive culture, not ones that will undermine the high values in the organization. The integrity edge manifests when a leader with a reputation for having integrity is more valued by exactly the sort of organization many of us desire to work in. Think about that for a moment: the very organizations most of us desire to work with—those with healthy cultures—tend to hire leaders who value integrity and trust. That can be a game changer. The integrity edge is often the *reason* leaders rise, not just how they rise.

Ethical leaders are remembered for how they led, not just what they accomplished. They leave behind healthier cultures and stronger people. They create a ripple effect by mentoring others, shaping culture, and influencing organizations long after they move on. Ethical leaders develop ethical leaders. This is the "shadow of a leader" effect Doug frequently referred to. The legacy of ethical leadership is generations of future leaders who value right action, trust, honesty, and service, and make choices that prove it.

THE ORGANIZATIONAL EDGE

Many years ago, I was a new manager on a global technology team. My team was responsible for approximately forty sites across North and South America. Almost immediately after being promoted to the manager role, I tasked Mark, a talented engineer on my team, to visit one of our California sites to help with a project that was not going well.

Mark completed the task and the project. Everything went well with the visit. But Mark and I struggled for months to develop a meaningful relationship. He was professional and respectful, but I had a hard time connecting with him.

As the years passed, Mark and I finally had a breakthrough, and our relationship grew to be one of my strongest at the company. I eventually asked him why it took us so long to connect. I clearly recall his almost reluctant answer: "Rusty, when you sent me to complete that project right after you became the manager, it was Valentine's Day."

Ok, I don't remember it being Valentine's Day, but why did that prevent us from forming a real relationship for so long?" I asked.

"I already had plans. I was going to ask my girlfriend to marry me that night. I already had the reservation and the ring. But you asked me to go to California," he answered.

"What? Why didn't you tell me? The project could have waited a few days."

"I didn't know you yet. I didn't know if I could do that. I didn't know how you would react. I mean, I know now. But I didn't know then," Mark replied.

Mark withheld very important feedback because he didn't trust me. In this case, trust was absent because we didn't know each other. It's a perfect illustration of how extremely valuable the integrity edge is for organizations.

The integrity edge brings remarkable benefits to the teams and organizations under its influence. At the heart of this impact is psychological safety. When leaders model integrity, teams feel safe to share the full truth—even when it is difficult to hear. There is no fear of retaliation or political maneuvering; team members trust that their leader values honesty over appeasement.

Teams thrive when they believe their leader invites honesty. When people speak up about problems early on, leaders can respond quickly, reducing risks and driving better solutions. In cultures grounded in integrity, engagement flourishes. As employees feel safe and supported, they tend to work harder, collaborate more openly, and invest in themselves because they feel respected and valued. Barriers between teams come down. Silos that usually separate departments dissolve when leaders foster open communication and authentic relationships. Trust becomes an organizational and social currency, strengthening bonds, reducing conflict, and encouraging mutual support. I have witnessed firsthand how ethical leadership turns groups of employees into high-functioning teams.

Integrity-driven leadership also fuels innovation. When employees trust that their leader will have their back, they take more risks. They stop playing defense and start thinking creatively. Leaders who reward thoughtful risk-taking create cultures where innovation is the norm, not the exception.

Loyalty and retention are natural byproducts of this approach. People want to work for leaders they respect, and they stay with organizations where they feel valued. High-integrity leaders often find that employees are willing to follow them from one opportunity to the next, trusting that the leader's presence signals a place worth investing in. Consider Doug again. Even the traumatic experience of being laid off did not dissuade Doug from wanting to work with me again. Can you believe that? Ethical organizations enjoy lower turnover, higher morale, and a steady stream of talented individuals drawn to a workplace where values are more than just words on a wall. That's the integrity edge.

Finally, organizations grounded in integrity build reputations that endure. Customers, partners, and stakeholders recognize the difference. Ethical decision-making leads to long-term success, avoiding the traps of short-term wins with damaging long-term consequences. Integrity creates organizations where employees thrive, customers trust, and partners want to collaborate. Cultures shaped by integrity become magnets for good people and good business.

THE ROAD LESS TRAVELED

With all these benefits, you'd think the integrity edge is a no-brainer, right? Choosing to lead in this way is not always easy. Let's be honest, shall we? Look around you, and you will see many leaders who are highly successful and have not chosen the path of integrity. It is so common, it's expected. It's the stereotypical self-absorbed, power-hungry, "my way or the highway" organizational leader. This is the stereotype because it is the common path—the path most traveled. Two roads diverge in the leadership world, and the integrity edge is at the end of the path less traveled.

Two roads diverge in the leadership world, and the integrity edge is at the end of the path less traveled.

One path tempts with fast results, smooth politics, and personal gain. The other asks more of you. It requires humility, service, and clarity about what really matters. That path—the one forged by character and sustained by trust—is the one that builds something worth having. It's the road less traveled, and it makes all the difference.

It's true that plenty of people succeed without integrity. But they often leave a wake—a trail of broken trust, exhausted teams, and missed potential. What they build rarely lasts. It crumbles under the weight of fear, ego, or self-interest. The integrity edge is different.

It's not just the moral choice—it's the strategic one. It gives you clarity, confidence, and peace of mind. It empowers your team in a way that cannot be replicated through fear or manipulation. It unlocks the kind of momentum that only trust can create. Yes, this path is more demanding. But it's also more fulfilling.

In what follows, we'll look at six obstacles to ethical leadership that could prevent you from growing a leadership career characterized by character, integrity, and trust. If you learn to recognize and avoid these stumbling blocks, you will lead with integrity and you will flourish with the integrity edge.

The Six Stumbling Blocks of
LEADERSHIP

1

A FOUNDATION OF TRUST

How to Build a Reputation That Inspires Loyalty
and Performance

> *"Leadership without mutual trust
> is a contradiction in terms."*
>
> — WARREN BENNIS, *leadership scholar and author of*
> On Becoming a Leader [iv]

TRUST IS THE CORNERSTONe of leadership. Ethical, service-centered leadership relies on a foundation of mutual trust between the leader and the team. Senior leaders experience the lack-of-trust stumbling block when they begin to devalue the importance of cultivating and encouraging trust within their organization. Trust is fragile. It seldom grows on its own. It must be cultivated with care and intention, or it withers. And once it's lost, rebuilding it is one of the most daunting tasks a leader can face.

In organizations where trust breaks down, something dangerous happens. Leaders begin to believe that control is the only path forward. They shift into command-and-control mode. They stop inviting collaboration and start issuing mandates. And teams, sensing the lack of trust, respond in kind, with guardedness, disengagement, and just enough effort to stay off the radar.

Leaders produce an effective countermeasure to the loss of trust when they treat it as an imperative and understand it is their responsibility to cultivate and protect trust within their sphere of influence. In this chapter, we will review specific actions and attitudes that will allow you to sidestep the lack-of-trust stumbling block.

Trust is a precondition for the integrity edge. The benefits of leading with integrity cannot happen unless there is trust. Let me repeat: It cannot happen. There is no scenario in which the integrity edge exists where trust does not thrive. Zero.

TRUST—BE WORTHY OF TRUST

There is a school of thought that suggests trust must be earned. I recommend that you do not enroll in this school. I understand why people hesitate. Many of us have been burned. We have been lied to, let down, or betrayed by someone we trusted. That pain leaves a mark. It teaches us to withhold trust until it's proven safe. That reaction is human, but if you're serious about leading with integrity, it's also a trap.

The "earn my trust first" mindset might protect you from disappointment, but it will also limit your ability to lead. It builds walls where you should be building bridges. It keeps you in a posture of control instead of service. That's why servant-minded leaders reject it. They don't let past pain dictate present posture. I urge anyone who desires to model servant-style leadership to see this mindset as a stumbling block.

If we hope to avoid the lack-of-trust stumbling block, we must trust our team members and act in a way that encourages them to trust us. This approach starts with shifting our default response from "you must earn my trust" to extending trust by default. Lead like you believe your team is honest, capable, and worthy of that trust. Most of them are. And for the few who prove otherwise, you'll deal with that when it happens. But you can't lead with integrity if your baseline assumption is skepticism. Of course, when someone breaks trust, it matters. It must be addressed. Ignoring it sends the message that integrity is optional. But letting one person's failure shape your posture toward everyone else? That creates a culture of guardedness and fear.

By treating people this way—extending trust by default—we establish a standard that our team members can emulate. Trusting by default encourages others to do the same.

It is important to understand that if a team member violates the trust of the leader or a coworker, the situation must be dealt with. As a leader, you cannot allow individuals who have proven themselves to be untrustworthy to mingle with your trusted team. I have heard some say that the culture of any team is largely determined by the worst behaviors the leader allows. To protect your team and prevent dishonest actions, leaders must not be passive. Direct and decisive action is required to prevent such an individual from tainting the trust you and your team are cultivating. You must protect the trust you have built.

A PREDETERMINED NONNEGOTIABLE

There is no faster way to destroy trust than by lying. It is a truly efficient trust killer. If your team learns they cannot believe the words you say, how can they possibly trust the actions you take? Nothing will undermine a leader's effort to build and protect a trusting culture faster than for the leader to be found lying.

Fortunately, there is a simple, 100 percent effective method to ensure your team never discovers you lied.

Don't lie. How simple is that? Just tell the truth, and the risk of being discovered in a lie decreases to 0 percent. That is a fantastic return on investment.

There is no faster way to destroy trust than by lying. It is a truly efficient trust killer.

It is critical that you predetermine honesty as a nonnegotiable. Few people, perhaps no one, have the willpower to construct their personal ethics and integrity standards when a decision is required. Imagine you have never considered how you feel about accepting a bribe until you're offered a significant sum of money for a favor. When you are offered the bribe, you have to decide how you will respond in the moment. The moment is so big, it could take over, and you are likely to take the path of least resistance. That is how humans operate. Unless you remove that path of least resistance for some specific, important reason, in that big moment, the easiest path will be very appealing.

Commit yourself to honesty. Commit yourself to treating big lies, white lies, exaggerations, tall tales, fishing stories—all of the untruths and half-truths—with contempt. Predetermining honesty as a nonnegotiable will help you avoid tempting situations where a half-truth would seem appropriate.

Being honest also means keeping your word. When you make a commitment, if you are honest, it means something to you. When you say yes, you should mean yes. When you say no, it should mean no. When you tell someone you will do something, or not, the honest person follows through with that claim.

Many leaders stumble on the lack-of-trust block when they stop considering the cost and implications of the commitments they make. They stop seeing the commitment as a promise. They begin using commitments as a conversation element, like discussing the weather and sports. Sure, they said they would call you back next week, but they didn't actually intend to call you back. It's just something people say. True. It is "just something people say" when they have no conviction about being honest and do not place an appropriate value on trust.

HOW (AND HOW NOT) TO CHANGE A COMMITMENT

Being honest and keeping your commitments does not mean you cannot change your mind or negotiate a different completion date. Every day we encounter surprises. Our perfectly laid plans meet unexpected new variables. The 19th-century military leader Helmuth von Moltke is credited with first stating, "No plan survives first contact with the enemy."[v] Many other military leaders have co-opted this saying. Perhaps more famously, Mike Tyson said, "Everyone has a plan until you get punched in the mouth."[vi] The point Mr. Tyson made so clear is that we can and should plan, but unexpected obstacles will do their best to interrupt our plans. At times we must change our plans. These changes will almost certainly result in changes to commitments we have already made. This is to be expected from time to time and, if done properly, will not constitute dishonesty.

In cases where unexpected variables interfere with our intention and force changes to our commitments, the changes must be made proactively, not retroactively. When we don't honor a commitment enough to at least inform or negotiate a needed adjustment, we are being dishonest. If you let a person know you changed your mind and did the thing you told them you would not do after you did it, that is dishonesty. That sort of action hastens the arrival of the lack-of-trust stumbling block.

HANDLING CONFIDENTIAL INFORMATION

Leaders are routinely brought into discussions about topics that are not ready to be shared broadly. Layoffs, acquisitions, salary negotiations, legal proceedings—the list goes on and on. Leaders are entrusted with confidential information as a normal course of business. Unless the information shared in this manner pertains to illegal activity, the leader is obligated to keep this information confidential. How does the honest leader respond when someone asks them if they know anything about a confidential subject?

Imagine you are a director at a three-thousand-employee healthcare organization in the United States. You are responsible for a team of thirty-five employees. As part of your normal responsibilities, you are brought into a discussion about the possibility that your organization will be acquired by a larger organization. Nothing is certain, but discussions are underway. One of your employees hears a rumor about a possible acquisition and asks you what you know about the rumor. Denying any knowledge of the discussions would be dishonest, and when it is discovered later, this dishonesty will erode the trust you have established with the employee who asked you what you know. However, you do not have permission to divulge what you know about these discussions. In fact, you do not have permission to acknowledge the discussions are even happening. How does an honest leader navigate a delicate situation like this?

The key to responding in this situation is to focus your response on how you would be required to act if you were in possession of information about the rumored discussions. You can respond honestly to the inquirer if you highlight what your responsibilities would be in situations like the employee is proposing. "If such conversations were happening and I were involved, I would be obligated to keep the discussions confidential. I have been involved in discussions like this in the past. Every time, participants are obligated to keep even the existence of such discussions confidential. As for this rumor, as soon as I know anything and am given permission to share it, I will let you know."

Your response should focus on your responsibilities in any hypothetical situation requiring confidentiality. The employee's curiosity may not be satisfied, but you have preserved the trust they have in you, and you haven't violated your confidentiality commitment.

OWNING UP TO YOUR MISTAKES

You are going to make mistakes. I suspect you knew that without me mentioning it. How we respond when we make mistakes reflects our honesty and impacts how trustworthy we appear to others. When we decide to deflect the results of our mistakes or fail to acknowledge when our missteps negatively impact others, we place tremendous pressure on the fragile trust we are building with our teams. In times like these, we run a heightened risk of hitting the lack-of-trust stumbling block.

Years ago, I was a leader in an early-stage technology company. My team had to create much of the company's technical assets from scratch—we started with nothing. Every element of the technical stack was being defined from the ground up. My team was lean (read: tiny) and moving fast.

My team had been reviewing contenders for a specific piece of technology for a couple of months. They did their research, opened trial accounts, worked with the tool, and documented their findings. They considered a wide range of factors, including ease of use, scalability, security, and costs. The leader of the small team made his recommendations and stated his case. I agreed with his recommendations. We got the legal team to help us review the sales order and service contract. Once all of the process steps were covered, I approved the purchase and executed the small contract.

Weeks passed and my team started familiarizing themselves with the new technology. My manager asked me about the status of the tool selection a couple of times, confirming my suspicions he did not know that I had already selected the tool and executed the first contract.

I should have immediately clarified the status, but I hadn't included him and the other executives in the decision. I knew that was an error. I avoided answering his questions about the status of the tool selection. I kept silent because I didn't want to admit I had completely ignored my manager's and peers' opinions in the selection process. I only considered the opinions of my team members and I realized how incomplete that approach was. There was little I could do about it after the fact, so I dragged my feet and continued to avoid revealing these mistakes to my manager. This went on for more than a month. My manager asked several times for a status update, and I continued to drag my feet.

I heard someone say many years ago, "Bad news ages like milk." That little phrase creates some fairly compelling imagery. In this case, my bad news was that I had already made a selection without considering the inputs of my peers and my manager. Over a month after I first dodged my manager's question, my tool selection decision was like three-month-old milk.

The charade finally ended when I wrote a remorseful email admitting to the decision and the ongoing deception and asking for my manager's understanding and forgiveness. The letter landed with predictable reception. My manager was appalled. He wasn't appalled by the decision—he did not have sufficient experience with our research or the tool marketplace to make this assessment. He was appalled by my lack of inclusion and weeks of withholding details from him. When we finally spoke, his disappointment was palpable, as was the undertone of tightly controlled fury.

I spent the next several weeks working through the activities I originally neglected to complete with my manager and peers. The joint selection activities resulted in the same decision my team made. I'd made the right choice, but how I handled the situation was among the worst mistakes of my career.

Ultimately, my manager was gracious and did not fire me—an outcome I was certain was possible, even likely. My attempt to diminish the impact of a mistake completely backfired. Had I admitted the mistake immediately, we would have gone through the selection process with my colleagues and ended up with the same choice. I would still have to admit the misstep to my peers as part of the process, but I would not have violated the trust I had built with my manager. I would not have risked my employment. I would have spared myself months of embarrassment and shame as I faced my manager, each day hoping I could rebuild some modicum of trust and respect with him.

When Bill Gates Messed Up

Each of us has a unique style and personality. We each bring a personal touch and the weight of our experiences to our leadership style. We have seen things that work well and things that do not work well firsthand. We have tried and failed, and we have tried and succeeded. Regardless of the length of your experience, you have developed a style and personal tendencies. The things we experience color our style and approach. Being authentic means being true to yourself—your style, personality, and beliefs—as you lead and inspire others. When a leader acts in ways that are not in agreement with these established characteristics, it can be seen as inauthentic.

At times, when a leader behaves inauthentically, their followers can find it confusing or awkward. If I lived to be one hundred years old, I suspect I would remember the Microsoft Windows 95 launch event clearly. It was in August of 1995. Microsoft had a worldwide release event. It was a global spectacle. There were live kickoff events all over the world. A level of energy and excitement surrounded the worldwide multimedia exhibition like no other technical product release had ever seen.

The main stage of this global kickoff was located at Microsoft's headquarters in Redmond, Washington. CEO and Cofounder Bill Gates shared the stage with Executive Vice President Steve Ballmer. Others were on the stage, but these gentlemen were the principal actors. Bill Gates was a reserved, focused, innovative technology pioneer, while Ballmer was known to be an energetic, enthusiastic leader. At the kickoff event, both danced around the main stage, pumping up the crowd in attendance. I recall thinking at that moment, and frequently since, that Bill Gates was uncomfortable with this outward display of excitement. I have never spoken to Mr. Gates; perhaps I am incorrect. But dancing and hyping up the crowd in that manner seemed at odds with the serious leader I had come to view him as. It did not cause me to trust him or Microsoft any less, but it did feel awkward and cheesy. If you have not already seen the event I am talking about, do yourself a favor and find the video online. It is one of the cringiest things you will view today, I promise.

At other times, however, being inauthentic can directly impact the trust followers have in a leader. Many years ago I worked in a technology group for a medium-sized, fast-growing company in the United States. The CEO was a smart, personable man with a reputation for caring deeply for the company, employees, and customers. In company meetings, he spoke passionately about the company mission and the important, positive impact the company had on so many people. He even teared up occasionally as the company's mission hit close to home for him, and he shared personal stories from his family's experience. He was a likable man who was trusted by most of the company. I did not know anyone at the company who thought ill of the CEO. Gradually, though, the CEO began acting contrary to the caring and compassionate persona he had cultivated. He made decisions that seemed incongruent with the personality he portrayed for years. He overtly protected and encouraged executives who chastised and berated subordinates in public. He stopped prioritizing employee engagement improvement programs. He established a pattern of terminating senior and mid-level managers just months before their bonuses and equity vested. This CEO's actions over several months were in stark contrast with the personality and approach so many of us had come to deeply trust. As a result, the CEO lost the trust of many—perhaps most—of his company far more quickly than he developed that trust. In this case, the inauthentic actions were not awkward or cheesy—they were trust-destroying.

Once established, a leader's style, personality, and beliefs form an image of who they are. Followers expect the leader to act in a certain way given a set of circumstances. The team begins to predict how they will act, and becomes curious when their actions do not align with what is expected. If the team doesn't understand why the misalignment happened, trust may be impacted.

This is not to say the leader cannot change over time. We all continue to have experiences that mold our personality and style. It is reasonable to expect some drift to take place. Or a leader may identify aspects of their personality or style that they are unsatisfied with. They can intentionally focus on making changes to how they lead. A leader might improve their communication style to be more effective or influential. They may intentionally engage employees to collect more direct feedback from their team members. A leader could become passionate about a cause they previously had no exposure to. In each of these cases, there is a clear explanation for the change. It is not inauthentic; it is personal growth. Personal growth in a leader will not erode trust. In fact, this sort of change can protect and encourage trust among the leader's staff members. They can appreciate a leader who is self-aware and interested in continuous improvement.

One symptom of being inauthentic that all leaders should watch out for—and that all employees seem to notice instinctively—is waffling. Waffling is when someone changes their mind frequently. It is when someone seems to have no convictions and changes their opinion each time they hear a new point of view or run into any resistance. It is okay to have a point of view and change it when new evidence is presented or you learn new facts or variables that weigh on your decision. More than okay, this is a sign of maturity and a desirable trait for the ethical leader. However, when your point of view changes every time you disagree with a person in a position of power, you are not being authentic. Authenticity sometimes requires you to stand your ground even when you disagree with someone in a position of power who has influence over you. To stand and say, "This is my belief. I know it is different from what you believe. Here are the reasons I believe this way"—that is what authenticity looks like.

DO AS YOU SEE ME DO

I suspect everyone reading this book has heard the phrase "leading by example." It's a catchy phrase and a powerful approach to service-minded leadership. However, there is a problem with the phrase "leading by example." It is not specific enough to be actionable. What does leading by example mean in our pursuit of career growth without compromise? I have recast the principle of "leading by example" as "modeling the behaviors you desire from your team." Show the team how they should act and react based on what you do and the things you focus on. Few things will sabotage your trust-building faster than leading in a "do as I say, not as I do" manner. This mode frustrated us when we were kids and heard it from our parents, and it still sets us off when we see people in positions of power taking a similar tack.

Instead, when we adopt a "do as you see me do and say as you hear me say" approach, we encourage trust and collaboration—two keys to effective leadership. Modeling the behaviors you desire from your team members means acting the way you want them to act, treating people the way you want them to treat people, and speaking to them the way you want them to speak to others. This is not to suggest we are trying to make puppets out of our team members. It is to establish the team's culture as demonstrated by the team's actions—starting with the team's leader. When an entire team places value on the same behaviors, a team culture is born. When they place value on behaviors that demonstrate trust, integrity, compassion, and service, an amazing culture capable of incredible things is born, and the embers of the integrity edge are stoked.

Few things will sabotage your trust-building faster than leading in a "do as I say, not as I do" manner.

WHEN THE GOING GETS TOUGH

This discipline starts with not requiring the team to do things you are unwilling to do. This is not the same as asking the team to do things you cannot do. There will be times, probably many of them, throughout your career when you will have specialists on your team that can do things you have never been able to do. It would be absurd to suggest that a leader should be an expert in every subject matter and discipline the team operates in. That is not the way teams work. An effective team is constructed of team members who create a sum greater than the parts. An effective team has members who complement one another—strengths to cover weaknesses.

Not requiring the team to do things you are unwilling to do means not having two sets of rules—one for the leader and one for the members. This is a trust-destroyer. For example:

- "Everyone is required to be in the office at 8 a.m." cannot mean "but the leader shows up at 10 a.m."
- "Everyone is required to work from the office at least three days a week" cannot mean "but the leader can work from home every day if they want."
- "Team members are expected to treat others with respect" cannot mean "but the leader can openly ridicule and chastise people in public without regard for how it might make that person feel."

If a rule is so onerous or unacceptable you will not follow it, why should your team be expected to follow it? When leaders exempt themselves from a rule, they tell the team they recognize the rule to be unacceptable but are unwilling to do anything to protect the team from the bad rule. Instead of protecting the team and challenging the rule, a poor leader claims authority to ignore it. However, by following the onerous rule, the leader models the behavior they desire from the team—following rules—and positions the leader to champion changes that improve the experience for all employees.

Sometimes, being willing to do something isn't about following a bad rule. Sometimes it is about doing what is required to get a job done. Some jobs require work to be performed in less-than-ideal conditions—in the heat, in the cold, in the rain, overnight, over weekends or holidays. In times like this, you can build your relationship with the team and encourage mutual trust by joining them in the less-than-ideal work conditions for a time.

If the team has to work in challenging weather conditions, join them. You do not have to join them for every minute of their challenging work, but show up and spend some time with them. If they are working in the heat, bring a cool, refreshing beverage to them when you arrive. If they are working in the cold, bring coffee. If they are working in the rain, well, there isn't much you can do to make them dry, so just show up and lend a hand. This recommendation will backfire unless the leader joins the team in the challenging conditions for more than a token moment. Candidly, the team will be encouraged if they see you are as uncomfortable as they are. That means putting yourself in the conditions for a time.

If the team has to work overnight or on the weekend, show up at the job site. Bring lunch for the team on Saturday. Stay and eat with them. Pop in during the overnight task with a snack or some fresh coffee. Stay with them for a while. Ask them how things are going and see if there is anything you can do to help with the work. If they share something you can do to help, do it. Do not just think or talk about helping. If you show up at inconvenient times and add value to the team, it will positively impact the team members. They will notice your actions and their trust in you will almost certainly grow.

DOING THE HARD THINGS

In leadership, sometimes you are presented with hard decisions that will impact people's lives regardless of your choice. You must be willing to embrace these hard decisions, not just eventually, reluctantly, or passively go along with whatever happens at the last moment. Effective, service-oriented leadership demands that leaders serve their team members.

When leaders see something that needs to be taken care of, they must deal with it decisively and promptly. Waiting for someone else to handle it, or hoping it will just pass, is not the leadership style we are looking for.

By way of example, I will share a particularly difficult decision I faced during my career in technology leadership. It has been said that a team's culture is largely determined by the worst behavior its leaders allow. If a leader allows team members to be disrespectful, the team will, in the long run, have a culture where disrespecting people is acceptable. When a leader does not enforce timeliness as a requirement, meetings will likely routinely start late and run long.

The converse is true, too. The behaviors a leader emphasizes will, over time, influence the culture of a team. As a leader, if you want a team that shows up to meetings on time, you should show up to meetings on time and hold team members accountable for the same. This sets a clear example for your team to follow. If a leader wants a team culture that prioritizes being respectful of one another, the leader must model that respectful behavior and correct disrespectful behavior when and where they see it.

Sometimes, enforcing the desired behaviors means taking actions you wish you could avoid. It might mean doing difficult or uncomfortable things because doing so preserves the culture you cultivate at your organization.

I had to make a difficult decision like this many years ago when I was leading a global technology team. My leaders and I had been working hard to instill a culture of honesty and respect in our company. We had intentionally focused on setting and keeping commitments with our business stakeholders to prove we could be trusted. If anyone in the technology team said something, the business could trust that it was true, even if they didn't understand the underlying technology. Establishing this sort of trust is critical if you desire to be an effective leader. To preserve the trust we fought so hard to build, we could not have any employees acting in an untrustworthy manner.

One morning I got a call from one of the subordinate leaders on my team. He informed me of a discovery he and his team made when completing a maintenance event at one of our data centers. His team discovered several personally-owned devices connected to the company's internet connection in the data center. Company policy and security best practices explicitly forbade devices of this nature. These devices represented a true security vulnerability to the company. Installing these devices in the company data center was an unquestionable misuse of company resources, given the company was paying for power, cooling, and internet connectivity for the data center. It would be like a delivery driver using the company truck to facilitate a personal side business making personal deliveries on the weekend—and doing so without permission. It would be like a surgeon using a hospital's operating room to perform surgeries related to a side-hustle business and doing so without the hospital's knowledge. It clearly misuses company assets and almost certainly opens the company up to security and legal risks.

In the ensuing investigation, we determined beyond a shadow of a doubt that these devices were the property of the smartest, hardest working, most creative engineer I have ever worked with. Essentially, we discovered that my best employee violated the company's trust. We discovered that an employee who was my "go-to guy" for every emergency situation and complex request had misused company resources for personal gain for months, perhaps even years.

At this point in the investigation, only a handful of the company employees knew of the incident, and fewer still knew who the guilty party was. I had a decision to make.

I had to take swift disciplinary action if honesty and trust were important to me, as I constantly claimed they were. However, If I wanted to keep the sharpest technical employee I had ever worked with on my team, I needed to find a way to sweep the entire incident under the rug as quickly and quietly as possible.

For the ethical leader, even though it's a difficult decision, the right choice is clear. There is no dilemma. Trust and honesty are more important than any individual, regardless of how important that individual is.

Before the end of that day, the employee was placed on administrative leave and his access to company resources was suspended. Several days later, when the forensic investigation was completed and the devices were definitively tied to the employee, he was terminated for cause.

I won't claim my commitment to trust and respect made this easy. I still had to terminate a friend. I still had to remove my best resource from my team. I still had to explain to the rest of my team and the company that I terminated one of my most-respected team members without divulging the details of the incident. It was not easy, but because I predetermined that trust and respect were nonnegotiable leadership principles on which our team and company culture were built, it was easier than it might have been. Leaders must be willing to do this to build and protect the right culture for their teams and their companies.

COMMIT, DO, REMIND

Keeping commitments is one of the behaviors that will build the most trust among team members and stakeholders. Modeling this behavior as a leader means accepting action items yourself, not just assigning action items to those who work for you. Take personal responsibility for tasks. When your team members see you publicly accepting and completing tasks, it underscores the importance of making and keeping commitments.

To maximize the impact keeping commitments has on building trust, consider the "commit, do, remind" process. This simple, repeatable process is designed to maximize the impact of completed commitments in trust building. It is particularly useful if the leader or team is initially building trust or is trying to repair a damaged relationship.

The process starts with an understanding that making commitments sets you up to improve your trust with the party you are committing to. The commitment needs to be specific—what you are saying you will do and when it will be completed. The commitment must not be vague. Commitments with specific scope and completion statements eliminate misinterpretations and maximize the impact of the completed commitment. It's the difference between how you feel when someone tells you, "I will get to it eventually," and how you feel when someone tells you, "I will complete 100% of that task no later than Friday at 4 p.m." The first provides no confidence and barely represents a commitment. The second is specific, a commitment I can be confident in. Think of the "commit" step in this process as investing in your trust bank with the other party. Each time you commit, you set up the possibility of delivering a positive return on your investment.

Once you have made the commitment, you must keep that commitment. This is the "do" step of the process. Do everything you can to keep the commitment. If the commitment is at risk, share why and what your plans are to mitigate the risk with anyone to whom you made the original commitment as soon as you are able. Changes and surprises happen. Timelines get impacted. People understand this. What people do not understand, and will strain any existing trust, is when you make a commitment and fail to deliver that commitment without explanation or update.

Once the commitment has been fulfilled, you are on to the "remind" step of the process. You completed the commitment; now share the results of the successfully completed commitment with the people to whom you originally made the commitment. Be sure to do so in a humble way. The point isn't to show off or grandstand, but to remind the stakeholders that you made a commitment and then kept it. This final step is important to underscore your trustworthiness. Some people will connect the dots without the reminder, but others will not. I find this final step in the "commit, do, remind" cycle to be important in maximizing the impact of the trustworthy action.

Commit

Making commitments creates the opportunity to increase trust.

Do

Following through on commitments creates trust.

Remind

Reminding the person that you kept your commitment maximizes the impact of trust built.

"Commit, do, remind" is a process that works best when it becomes part of your standard leadership approach. You become the leader who makes specific commitments and keeps them. People who work with you begin to expect you to volunteer to complete a task, and once you agree, they have confidence that you will complete it.

Trust does not happen automatically. It grows with intentional action. It must be cultivated—like a garden. The "commit, do, remind" process allows you to create opportunities to positively impact your trust with team members and stakeholders. Using this process to plant the seeds of trust will result in an integrity edge harvest.

CONTINUOUS LEARNING

Continuous learning is not just about acquiring new knowledge. It is about acknowledging that you have more to learn, that you do not know it all, and that you value other people's input and points of view. For the leader, continuous learning is about cultivating a leadership style that values growth, collaboration, and openness. These principles are foundational to building trust within a team. Demonstrating, through your actions, that you are a continuous learner paves the way for your team to do the same.

When leaders share what they study, they highlight their humility and growth mindset. If the leader were infallible and knew it all, they would have no need for additional learning. By sharing what you are learning, you show that you believe people can grow and you know you have more to learn. Moreover, when you share the knowledge you gain during your studies, you encourage others to share what they have learned. You cultivate a team dynamic that values keeping an open mind, filling your open mind with new ideas, and sharing those ideas with your team members.

EXTREME OWNERSHIP

Demonstrating ownership is a powerful behavior to model as you develop your high-character leadership approach and grow your career. In the book *Extreme Ownership*, two former Navy Seals argue that a leader's responsibility is to take full ownership of their team, their mission, and the outcomes of their actions. They state that leaders must own everything in their sphere of influence and, by doing so, eliminate all finger-pointing and excuses. If something happens while you are in charge, the outcome is your responsibility. This principle, which they call "extreme ownership," develops a culture of accountability and builds trust within teams. [vii]

For most of my career, I have been responsible for technology systems—the applications, data centers, servers, and storage that the world runs on. Technology systems, like automobiles, aircraft, and lawnmowers, require routine maintenance. For technology systems, this routine maintenance is typically scheduled during hours when the systems are not heavily used (read: in the middle of the night).

During one such maintenance event many years ago, I had the opportunity to demonstrate my understanding and practice of extreme ownership.

During this maintenance event, we were working on a critical system. The maintenance proceeded as expected for the first several hours; there were no surprises. The team worked overnight to install patches and security fixes to the critical system. After several hours, with the patches installed, it was time to bring the systems back online, but something went wrong.

When the engineer who performed the maintenance attempted to bring the critical systems back online, they did not restart like they were supposed to. At this point, many hours into the maintenance event, they had to troubleshoot how to get the system back online. This troubleshooting took several hours. They recovered the system to approximately 80 percent of full operating capability. Some system processes could not be recovered after the maintenance event.

Why weren't they able to recover the system to 100 percent capability? During the course of the recovery, the team discovered that they did not have current backups for this system. They had backups, but there had been changes to the system that were not represented in the backups. The last usable backups had been created before the last system changes. There was nothing the team could do to recover the missing configuration data. The backups simply did not exist.

For this particular critical system, not having current, usable backups was a catastrophic finding. There were applications that relied on this configuration information that simply wouldn't work unless the system was recovered to its former state. The configuration could not be recreated. This system possessed advanced security features that were designed to prevent this sort of configuration change. The original state must be restored from the backup or it could not be restored.

HOW COULD THIS HAPPEN?

My team had detailed disaster recovery policies and procedures. These policies and procedures outlined the backup requirements for all critical systems. Our procedures called for the backups of any critical systems to be verified prior to the start of any maintenance event involving a critical system.

Per the policy, the engineer should have tested the backups prior to starting the maintenance event and, when he discovered the gap in coverage, he should have canceled the maintenance event. This was the disaster recovery policy and the maintenance change procedure. He did not follow the established procedures.

When he discovered the gap in the backups, he immediately knew the implications of this finding. He escalated to his director and coworkers immediately. Together, they were able to restore 80 percent of the critical system's functionality, but there was nothing to be done for the remaining capabilities. This recovery would be manual, messy, and would take weeks—perhaps months—to complete. The director who was responsible for the team informed me of the state of the systems and the outcome of the maintenance events the following morning.

After getting up to speed on the events of the previous evening and the state of the critical system, the director and I had to make a decision. How would we take ownership of the maintenance outcome? Who was ultimately responsible for the failed maintenance event? Did we believe that leaders have responsibility for all the outcomes that occur during their tenure or not?

This engineer made a mistake. He should have checked for current backups before starting the scheduled maintenance. He didn't. He was clearly responsible for the poor outcome, right? What about the principle that leaders have ownership of everything that happens under their watch? How could the leader be responsible for confirming the backup before an event in which he was not involved?

The leader is responsible because they are the ones who need to impress upon the engineer why the procedure of verifying the backup prior to the maintenance event is so important. The criticality of this particular system should have been impressed upon that engineer more completely.

Think about how surgeons and surgical teams prepare for complex surgeries—say, a heart transplant. I am not a surgeon and did not interview a surgeon while preparing this section, but I have watched my fair share of medical dramas. Based on that expertise, I can tell you that before the heart transplant, everybody who will be in the operating room and much of the support staff who will not be in the operating room, know exactly what their responsibility is. They have rehearsed the phases of the operation. They understand the steps completely. They understand the contingencies. They understand the circumstances, if present, that will require the surgery to stop. Everybody in the room understands it's life and death. The entire team understands these things because the surgery leader ensures that they walk through it. The surgeon makes certain they appreciate the gravity of the situation. The surgeon knows that if one of the team members does not follow the established procedures, the outcome could be catastrophic. So, they focus on communication and training prior to the surgery, ensuring the team is prepared and informed.

In the case of the failed maintenance event, this engineer didn't have an appreciation for the criticality of the system. Had he understood how critical that system was, he would have been hyper-aware of the importance of the backup. I would argue that if the director and I had done our jobs properly and trained the team on how important this system was to operations, there would have been a fair amount of fear and apprehension in that engineer before starting the maintenance event. That fear would manifest as respect for the backup procedure and would have ensured that he followed the process. Instead, we didn't impress upon him the critical nature of the system, and as a result, he skipped steps in the procedure. The engineer has some culpability, but if his leaders had done their job properly, he would have been better trained and better prepared to complete the maintenance of this critical system.

During the meeting with the director in the morning after the failed maintenance event, I told the director I did not want to know the engineer's name. There were only three or four engineers that it could have been, but I decided not to learn the engineer's identity. I realized that it could have been any of the engineers. This failed maintenance event was more an outcome of the director and me failing to prepare the team than it was the engineer's failure to follow the procedure. I didn't ask for the engineer's identity, and when my boss asked me, I told him I was not prepared to share that name because the failure was on me and my director as much as it was on the engineer. If I shared the engineer's name, I was concerned he might be made a scapegoat for this error, which was an outcome I could not support. The director and I bore the responsibility for the failure, and over the next couple of months, we were able to get all systems back to an operational state. During that same time, we also improved our training on backup procedures. This wasn't a mistake that was going to happen again.

The path the director and I took in the aftermath of the failed maintenance event exemplifies extreme ownership. Perhaps it seems too extreme. Perhaps you are reading this and thinking it was foolish of me and my director to protect the engineer who made the mistake. However, consider what we could have done before the maintenance event that could have changed the outcome. If the director and I had been more intentional about training the team on proper maintenance procedures and the critical nature of this system in particular, the engineer would have been better prepared to execute the maintenance activities. If the leader can influence the outcome, they have an obligation to do so.

If the leader can influence the outcome, they have an obligation to do so.

Our silence on the training and criticality amounted to leadership malpractice. Sure, we could have stuck the blame on the engineer and disciplined him, or even fired him if it came to that. But such an action would have been counterproductive. It would have taught all the engineers a lesson that they are on their own. It would show the engineers that if they make mistakes, they will pay for them. Instead, the approach we took showed the team that they were protected. It showed the team that their leaders were not above reproach and were willing to own the bad outcomes. It showed the team members an example of ownership they could emulate.

SUMMARY

Trust is the cornerstone of leadership. Most ethical leadership relies on a foundation of mutual trust between the leader and the team. Trust is fragile. If it is not purposefully developed and nurtured, it will die. Once trust dies in an organization, it is difficult to regrow. Senior leaders experience the lack-of-trust stumbling block when they begin to devalue the importance of cultivating and encouraging trust in their organization.

Trusting your team members, and being trustworthy yourself, can help you avoid the lack-of-trust stumbling block and provide access to the integrity edge. Being honest and authentic will also help you build and protect trust within your team. Leading by example and modeling the behaviors you desire from your team members will establish a culture that cultivates and supports trust among team members and stakeholders.

Actions you should take to encourage and protect trust in your team:

- Default to trust
- Protect trust
- Commit to honesty
- Negotiate commitments proactively
- Keep confidentiality
- Admit mistakes
- Be authentic in disagreement
- Commit to one set of rules
- Show up
- Do the hard things quickly
- Commit, do, remind
- Lead in learning
- Model ownership

2

THE PRIDE TRAP

When Confidence Becomes Arrogance— and How to Avoid the Fall

"The best leaders are humble enough to realize their victories depend upon their people"

—JOHN C. MAXWELL, *leadership expert and author of* The 21 Irrefutable Laws of Leadership [viii]

AS LEADERS ACHIEVE MORE, gain titles and power, and grow confident in their abilities, their perspective often shifts. They may start to feel entitled to special treatment and recognition. Gradually, their focus can drift from supporting and uplifting their team to emphasizing their own significance within the organization. Leadership begins to center less on empowering others and more on seeking opportunities to highlight personal achievements. This growing sense of pride can become a barrier—a stumbling block—leading leaders away from the principles of ethical growth and collective success.

I was recently reminded of a near tragic encounter that could have been completely avoided had the leader acted with more humility. On a foggy night in late spring, the USS *Resolute* was navigating the northern Atlantic waters off Newfoundland's coast. The USS *Resolute* was one of the largest warships in the United States Atlantic fleet. Just after 4 a.m. on that fateful morning, the radar operator on the USS *Resolute* identified an unknown surface contact several miles out from the ship, but approaching on a collision course. The radar operator notified the first officer immediately. After assessing the situation, the first officer established radio contact with the unknown vessel.

"Unidentified vessel, this is the USS *Resolute*. We have identified a potential collision course on our current trajectories. Recommend you alter your heading by 15 degrees starboard to ensure safe passage. Over."

After a few tense moments, the first officer heard the response, "USS *Resolute*, we confirm the potential collision course of your current trajectory and recommend you divert your course 15 degrees to port to avoid collision. Over."

The first officer was astonished. How could this vessel believe the USS *Resolute* would alter course to accommodate their insignificant vessel? Rather than engage with the clueless contact, the first officer called the captain to the bridge for his assessment. When the first officer briefed the captain, the captain was incensed.

"How dare they! They will change their course—I guarantee it," the captain said as he grabbed the radio microphone. "Unknown vessel, you are on a collision course with the USS *Resolute*. I say again, divert your course."

The unknown contact responded immediately, "USS *Resolute*. I heard your demand, but I will not be diverting our course. I recommend you divert your course 15 degrees to port immediately to avoid a collision. Over."

At this point, the captain was livid: "Unknown vessel. This is the captain of the USS *Resolute*, the largest warship in the North Atlantic and the third-largest ship in the United States fleet. We are accompanied by six additional warships and numerous support vessels. I demand that you immediately change your course 15 degrees starboard. Failure to comply immediately will force me to take decisive and effective steps to ensure the safety of this ship. You will not like the decisive steps I take! I assure you: you do not want to test me."

The seconds ticked by, and the tension grew. Just before the captain called the ship to General Quarters, the bridge heard, "USS *Resolute*, this is the lighthouse operator. Do what you feel you need to do. Out."

This was not a real encounter. Nevertheless, this is the sort of encounter that might be possible given how some leaders are governed by pride. Perhaps you know a leader who says things like, "Do you know who I am?" or, "I'm the boss, I don't do that sort of thing anymore. We have people to do those things." Or perhaps the classic, "If I wanted you to have an opinion, I would have given you one. Just do what you are told." These are statements made by leaders who have been derailed by the pride stumbling block.

THE PRIDE STUMBLING BLOCK

The pride stumbling block is among the most infectious stumbling blocks. Leaders who stumble on pride will almost certainly be challenged by other stumbling blocks. Pride takes the focus off the team and places it on the leader. Once the focus changes in this manner, the leader loses the ability to see and serve their team, as well as the desire to do so. Eventually, they stop believing the team is able to add any real value as they begin to embrace that they—the leader—are the source of real value. This is the breeding ground for many of the stumbling blocks.

The cure for pride is humility. Pride says, "Look at me," while humility says, "They did the work; look at them."

Focusing on remaining humble prevents pride from taking a foothold in your mind and actions. Staying humble is a qualification for the integrity edge.

The cure for pride is humility. Pride says, "Look at me," while humility says, "They did the work; look at them."

Pride and humility are not mutually exclusive.

The pride stumbling block describes the pride of a leader who feels superior and entitled and acts according to that entitlement. This kind of pride accepts all of the accolades for performance and growth but denies any blame for setbacks. Arrogance and aloofness characterize the pride stumbling block. This destructive pride is convinced of its preeminence and the inferiority of those "beneath" it. With this sort of pride, there is no humility. Humble is the antithesis of destructive pride.

However, there is a healthy, proper pride that is not destructive. Pride in accomplishments, group efforts, and others' achievements—this is healthy pride.

Notice the difference in the following statements. Some statements are from a leader with healthy pride, while others are from a leader exhibiting destructive pride.

- I am proud of what we accomplished this year. Everyone put in tremendous effort, and the results reflect that.
- I led this team to the best quarter we have ever had. My plan worked flawlessly.
- While we can be proud of this accomplishment, we can all agree there is room for improvement.

- This project failed because of those idiots in marketing. We would have been successful if they had done half as much work as I did.
- I am honored to accept this promotion. I am grateful for your trust in me, and I am excited to keep learning and growing as I take on this new challenge.
- Of course, I got the promotion. I was clearly the most qualified person for the job. It wasn't even close.

When our pride is in "us" and "we" rather than "me" and "I," it is more likely to be healthy. Appropriate, healthy pride acknowledges growth, learning, and collaboration. People with destructive pride focus on themselves, how deserving they are, and how great they are compared to others.

Remaining humble as your career, title, power, and compensation grows does not happen automatically. As your career grows, your influence on the lives and careers of others does too. As your influence increases, you will likely be surrounded by people who are happy to tell you how great you are. Some of those singing your praises will be honest and sincere and truly value you and your approach. Others will sing your praises to garner favor and consideration. Regardless, both types of admirers can have an inflating effect on your ego. Unless you take consistent, preemptive counteraction, you risk stumbling on the pride block.

YOU DIDN'T CLIMB ALONE

One strategy you can adopt to avoid the pride stumbling block is acknowledging that your successful career has not been a solo endeavor. Throughout the years that have brought you to this point in your career, you have had help.

You were part of a team during the journey. You had mentors and coaches. You had managers who championed you, teachers who taught you, and peers who encouraged you. No person is an island, and no leader advances alone.

As I look back at my career, several moments stand out as examples of when I received help from others. My first management job was offered to me without me even applying for it. In 2000, the world had just gotten over the Y2K scare, and I was a senior system engineer at a semiconductor company. I had only been with the company for a few months when I was called into the office of my manager's boss. My manager and his manager were sitting at the table. My manager's boss addressed me first, saying, "John has decided to leave the company in the next several weeks. He suggested I promote you to manage his team when he is gone."

If John had not championed me for the role and Veronica had not accepted John's recommendation, I would not have gotten my first management role. Perhaps I would have applied for the role when it was posted, but I had only been at the company for a few months. I doubt I would have decided to apply, and I am not certain I would have been considered if I had. I was simply too new. Nevertheless, because of the actions of John and Veronica, my management career started that day.

Remembering this story, and John and Veronica's impact on my career, helps me remain humble. There was nothing I could have done to make myself manager at that time, but they did it without my involvement.

Many years later, a similar situation occurred. I was a new employee at a software company in Texas. I had been in my senior manager role for less than four months. My director and his vice president called me into the office for a discussion. The vice president told me my director was taking a different role at the company and recommended me as his replacement. No application. No interview. No competition. There is nothing I could have done to get this promotion on my own. However, because of the actions of the director and vice president, I received a promotion that set me up on a path to continue my career growth.

In both examples, other people played prominent roles in advancing my career. Remembering these stories and their impact on my career helps ground me. I don't know where my career would be today if not for the actions of these four influential leaders in the early days. By acknowledging their impact, I protect myself from becoming too prideful and deluding myself into believing that "I got here on my own" and "nobody ever helped me." I remember these stories, and it helps keep me from saying, "Do you know who I am?" Because I know. I am the guy that John, Veronica, the director, and the vice president helped advance when I could not do it on my own.

Sure, you could say that these opportunities would not have come my way if I had not performed well in my job—that is true. But I know people who perform well in their jobs daily, month after month, year after year, but have not experienced this sort of surprise promotion. Other people with similar education, ability, and performance have not advanced like I did because they were not given the opportunities I was given. Opportunities are a little like luck—there isn't a lot I can do to make them happen. I can network with the right people, work hard, perform well, and do my job better than my peers, but if the opportunity to advance doesn't present itself, short of leaving my role and looking for a new one, there isn't a lot I can do. Keeping this in mind should help you maintain an attitude of gratitude.

MEET THE OTHER STARS

Have you heard the saying, "We are all stars of our own stories"? The saying conveys that we see the world through our unique perspective and have a sense of agency in how our stories are told. We have influence. In fact, as the stars of our stories, we tend to have the most influence on the stories of our lives. This concept can lead to a healthy, motivating mindset. Recognizing your ability to impact outcomes in your life, and your responsibility for what you do and do not do, is a healthy way to live.

But there is a danger in being the star of your story. When the story you tell yourself always revolves around you, it can lead to a self-absorbed, prideful attitude that discredits the value and impact of others. You want to adopt the powerful motivation that comes with being the star of your story, but you want to avoid dismissing other actors.

How can you learn to place a higher value on the other actors in your story?

Start by building relationships with them. When you know their stories, it is harder to dismiss the other actors. Reach out to your peers within the organization where you work. Don't just reach out to your peers in your own discipline. Cast a wider net. If you are in human resources, reach out to peers in sales, finance, and engineering. What you want to establish is a deeper understanding of all of the things that need to happen in your organization to keep it running well. This context will be helpful for several reasons.

1. The big picture provides context to your story. Gaining a deeper understanding of the entire system will encourage humility by highlighting all of the things you are not involved in.

2. Learning about the other functions in the company will help you understand the interconnectedness of the business functions. As an ancillary benefit, this understanding can help you deliver more meaningful service improvements, thereby increasing your team's value to the organization.

3. Thinking about other people—their successes, challenges, and aspirations—will help prevent you from becoming self-absorbed and dismissive of their importance. Thinking about other people with a positive, supportive, and appreciative frame of mind is a catalyst for the integrity edge.

The onset of unhealthy pride occurs when you undervalue others—their accomplishments, inputs, points of view, and challenges—and overvalue your accomplishments and points of view. Getting a deeper appreciation for the other "stars" at the company will help you stay humble.

WHAT SERVING OTHERS LOOKS LIKE

Serving others will have a greater impact on your ability to avoid unhealthy pride than anything else you can do. Serving can take many different forms. At times, it literally means acquiring and providing resources to others. At other times, however, it could mean advocating for others, finding ways to alleviate stressors, or tackling particularly difficult tasks. In every case, serving means improving the lives of those you serve.

Years ago, a young leader I remember demonstrated this trait in serving his coworkers at a new-hire offsite in Houston. I had just started working for a global telecom company. The department I worked for was a new business line the telecom company had recently acquired. The department still had the culture and traditions of the scrappy startup it had been before the acquisition. One of the department's traditions was to have a three-day, off-site event for all new hires in the first thirty days of their employment. This offsite was held in a camp-like setting in the suburbs of Houston. Over the three days, the new employees learned about the company's history, policies, and procedures, heard from the company president, and participated in many team-building activities.

One of these activities was a day of team-focused challenges on an obstacle course that small groups of five to eight employees would have to work together to navigate. There were no assigned leaders in the small groups. The groups were left to self-organize. In my group, one of the members was a particularly outspoken young guy who helped organize our team for each obstacle. He wasn't overbearing. He spoke up first, encouraged the team to share thoughts, and helped get and keep the team moving to solve the obstacles. Even though he was not named the team's leader, he quickly stepped into that role, and, mostly because of his effectiveness, the rest of the group eagerly followed his leadership.

The obstacle course included perhaps five or six challenges. By the time our group reached the second obstacle, the members had already fallen into a comfortable and cooperative rhythm that proved very effective. We completed the first, second, and third obstacles with some challenges, but each obstacle's outcome was never in doubt. The team was rolling. The young man's effectiveness as a leader was evident to everyone involved. So much so that the facilitator placed a new condition on the guy for the fourth obstacle. For the fourth obstacle, the

young man—the de facto leader of the team and the orga-
nizer of our success for the first three obstacles—was not
allowed to talk. The facilitator wanted others to step into
the gap and show their abilities. I suspect you can imagine
how this new tax was met by the team members. There
was mock outrage—how unfair it was, they were penal-
izing us because we were crushing their course, the facili-
tators were cheating, all of the usual suspects. Ultimately,
the new condition held, and the young man was muted for
the obstacle.

The fourth obstacle proved to be particularly messy.
While I don't recall every aspect of the activity now,
more than twenty-five years later, I do recall it involved
traversing a muddy pit, climbing structures with no convenient handholds from ground level, and, for reasons I
cannot recall, some kneeling and crawling around in the
muddy pit. Like the other obstacles, this one required
the team members to work together to successfully navigate it.

Since our vocal leader had lost his voice, others stepped
into the role, guided the discussion on how we would
navigate the trial, and organized the team members.
Throughout the discussion, the young leader stayed silent.

When the discussion was completed and the approach
was determined, the young man showed true leadership.
Without a voice to leverage his natural leadership tendencies, he was left to add value in other ways. This is
why when the team started their assault on the messy,
muddy pit, the young leader put himself in the nastiest
roles without discussion or delay. At times he offered his
hands and knees to help others traverse tall structures.
At another point, he moved first when someone had to
attempt to traverse the muddy pit to reach a required
element on the other side. But the most memorable task

that he volunteered for—mind you, volunteered with his actions, not his words—was when he got on his hands and knees in the mud to allow other team members to climb across his back to complete a specific aspect of the course.

When this leader couldn't use his voice—his primary tool for leadership and value—he identified other ways to add value to the team, and did those things without delay or being asked. He saw ways to serve the team and stepped into the gap. At the end of each obstacle, the facilitator held a short debrief where the team discussed lessons learned: what went well, what didn't go well, and a time for open discussion. During that debrief, several team members commented how, even without his voice, this leader found ways to lead and serve. They half-jokingly complained that the facilitator still cheated, but it didn't matter because the young man found ways to serve the team and make a difference.

This young leader demonstrated by his actions that service takes many forms. At the start of the day, he served by organizing discussions, motivating the team members, encouraging the team to keep moving, and anchoring the team when things got tough. However, by the fourth obstacle, his service took a completely different form. He served his team members physically by going places they couldn't or didn't want to go. He served them by taking on unfavorable conditions so they didn't have to. He understood that service is about providing the things the team needs to accomplish their tasks, no matter what those things might be.

When you consider how you can serve, don't limit yourself. Instead, "Focus, Listen, and Act."

FOCUS, LISTEN, ACT

Start by *focusing on the team members.* This might be the most impactful step in serving others and preventing unhealthy pride. Service starts by focusing on other people. Change your focus from what you need from the team to what the team needs from you. It is a 180-degree change from what prideful leaders do. Concentrate on finding the things that are encumbering them and determining how you can remove those barriers.

Now that you are focusing on the team members, *it is time to listen to what they are telling you.* Ask them questions about their jobs. What is working well? What is not working well? What obstacles are they dealing with today? What obstacles do they deal with routinely? What would improve their production, efficiency, engagement, or happiness? What is blocking their most urgent tasks from being completed? Ask them questions and then listen to what they say.

When you listen, force yourself to listen deeply to what they tell you. Their answers will be colored with their opinions and their point of view. However, their answers will provide great insights into what creates friction for them. When listening, refrain from casting aspersions or reframing their concerns to your point of view. Look for the tension in the story they are telling rather than forcing their story into your narrative.

Is there something in their answers that you can impact? Did you hear something that's causing them grief and that you can help change?

If you hear something, do something. *Act on the things you can influence.* The team has given you a gift by telling you what is causing them stress. Do not waste the gift. If you can do something about it, you should.

Focus on the team. Listen to what they are dealing with. Act in a way that makes their lives better.

THE HABITS OF RECOGNITION

We previously discussed the value of shifting the focus from self to others. This approach helps you avoid becoming self-absorbed and adopting unhealthy pride. That's a good start, but there is a way to take it to a higher level. Now that your focus is on other people, you can increase the benefit by purposefully recognizing their efforts and accomplishments.

Cultivating a habit of seeing and commenting on other people's work is a great way to maintain a healthy appreciation for the collaboration and teamwork required to be successful. It also carries the added benefit of being a fantastic motivator and helping keep team members engaged. The best recognition habits are multifaceted and intentional. Consider adopting an intentional recognition program designed around three F's: Format, Frequency, and Focus.

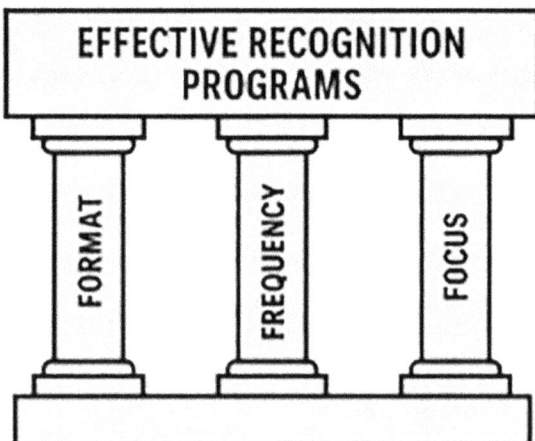

EFFECTIVE RECOGNITION PROGRAMS

FORMAT · FREQUENCY · FOCUS

Format

Effective recognition comes in many formats. Some recognition programs focus on formal, semi-annual recognition that collects nominations, and awards the most impressive or deserving nominees in a high-visibility ceremony. These are great programs. But effective recognition doesn't always have to be a formal, winner-take-all competition. Varying the format of the recognition you are giving can increase the effect the program has on your team members' engagement and on your efforts to remain humble.

Add instant messages, emails, texts, short conversations, and handwritten notes for more instantaneous recognition, along with the formal ceremonies, to get the maximum impact out of your recognition efforts. Not every team member will appreciate the attention and fanfare of a large-format recognition ceremony. For some team members, receiving a Slack or MS Teams message from a coworker or manager letting them know they are seen and their excellent results are recognized and appreciated is more meaningful. When you hear of a great outcome or a noteworthy effort or accomplishment, immediately reach out to the subject of the recognition and let them know you heard about the good things they are doing. The message does not have to be lengthy. You just want to tell the team member that you heard of their great work and that you appreciate their commitment and execution. Make it personal. Make it fun.

Sometimes I start instant message recognitions off with, "I heard what you did." Oftentimes, the recipient is not accustomed to having one-on-one conversations with the group's leader. A message from the boss is a surprise. And a message that starts off so ambiguous as to be almost ominous can be a memorable way of kicking off the recognition. Now, if you adopt this approach, it is vital that you immediately give up the charade and let the team member know what you heard is something good. Since the boss could be reaching out to chastise the team member for a mistake, drawing out the suspense is no fun. Use it as an ice-breaker. Do not use the maneuver to be cruel.

Be specific in your message. What did you hear? Who told you? What is it that you are impressed with? Generic "thanks for your great work" messages do not carry the same impact as "I heard you delivered a great presentation to our customer this morning. Sally told me that you prepared for that presentation for the last week, completed several rehearsals, and sought her feedback before the customer presentation. Sally said you thought of everything and wowed the customer." Can you see how a specific recognition is more impactful than a generic "way to go"?

For maximum impact on the team member, consider an old-fashioned, handwritten thank-you letter mailed to their home. This method can be more meaningful for three reasons.

1. First, how often do you receive mail delivered to your house that interests you? I don't mean your Amazon purchases. I mean snail-mail from someone you actually want to hear from. Perhaps on birthdays and holidays, but how often do you get a thank-you note out of the blue? I would guess, like me, it is fairly rare. The rarity increases the impact.
2. Secondly, handwritten notes take time to prepare, and the team member will recognize this. There is no way to mass-produce actual, handwritten notes. The leader must sit down, pen in hand, and focus on the team member's actions and impact. The

recipient will realize that the handwritten note took personal investment from the leader, and it should have a greater impact because of this.

3. Finally, when you send the thank-you note to the team member's home, their family sees the note. Their partner or child might even retrieve the note from the mailbox. When an employee receives a Slack message at work, they might tell their partner about it when they get home. Will they tell their children? Unlikely. But when the recognition is delivered to the employee's home, the likelihood that the people the employee cares most about are involved in the recognition increases dramatically. By sending the letter to the employee's home, the leader provides the possibility that the employee's family might become part of the recognition process. They might hear something like, "Dad, your boss really thinks you are doing a great job," "I am proud of you," or "Mom, I didn't realize you were so good at your job." You cannot buy that sort of impact, but you can get it for free if you take the time.

By leveraging multiple formats, your recognition program will be more effective. You will be able to engage each team member with the format they prefer and you will increase your reach and impact.

Frequency

Effective recognition programs have an appropriate frequency of activities. A recognition program that highlights accomplishments four times a year might not be as effective at motivating and encouraging team members as a program with more touch points. Also, the impact that a less-frequent recognition program has on preventing unhealthy pride is questionable, as the pride-squashing power of recognition is that it reminds the leader of the great things other people are doing. Recognition programs cause the leader to focus on other people and their accomplishments. This is how recognition programs help keep pride in check. As such, the most effective recognition programs include touch points with greater frequency.

Augment the semi-annual, formal recognitions with informal and spontaneous recognitions. I recommend making employee recognition a topic of every team meeting you hold and encouraging your team members to focus their attention on recognizing the effort, attitude, and outcomes of their coworkers. Make recognition a full team effort.

If you have properly structured your intentional recognition efforts, you are talking about recognition with team members and other leaders each week. You are hearing from your team about what they have seen others doing well. And you are reaching out to team members and members of other teams to tell them you know about the great work they are doing. A properly formatted recognition program becomes part of the team culture and can be a powerful way to encourage collaboration and teamwork.

Focus

The final "F" is focus. What elements of the employees' performance are you recognizing? Too often, recognition programs focus on what I call "heroic effort." For example, the semi-annual award goes to the team that worked eighty hours a week for three months to complete a project, or to Jack, who worked over the Thanksgiving holiday to fulfill a client commitment. "Heroic effort" is great, but is not the only recognition-worthy behavior we should applaud. Our recognition program should cast a wider net and include a more diverse range of behaviors to be more effective.

The truth is, recognition programs are partially selfish. Sure, you want the employee to know that you see the good work they are doing. And we certainly want the employees to be more engaged and happier about their work. These are certainly some of the benefits of recognizing employees. However, we also want to recognize employees to highlight the behaviors we want from all of our employees. Recognizing a particular behavior endorses that behavior as a desirable trait. Recognition says, "We value employees who do things like this at our company." Other employees see this and infer which behaviors they should be exhibiting to succeed on the team. With this in mind, it is easy to see why focusing only on "heroic effort" will result in an ineffective program.

Try tying your recognition focus to your company value statements. Most companies have prepared a list of core values or behaviors they believe are important. These company core value statements commonly include things like honesty, collaboration, innovation, customer focus, and communication. Consider selecting a different company value as the focus for your monthly recognition. When you discuss recognition with your team members and leaders, ask them to keep their eyes open for employees living out the focus value of the month. You won't always get great examples of every value every month. However, you will find far more examples when you focus on these values than if you do not. This intentional consideration will allow you to expand your recognition beyond "heroic effort" to include all behaviors you hope your team will emulate.

Recognition isn't just a feel-good gesture, it's a leadership habit that shapes culture, reinforces values, and fuels engagement. When done well, it keeps your focus on others, reminds you that success is a team sport, and creates an environment where excellence is seen and celebrated. By being intentional with the *format, frequency,* and *focus* of your recognition efforts, you do more than reward performance—you teach your team what matters most. In the process, you build a culture where the right behaviors are repeated, the right values are amplified, and the right people stick around.

STAY ACCOUNTABLE WITH A MENTOR

As leaders climb the corporate ladder, they gain power, influence, and prestige. With each promotion, they carry more responsibility and authority. With each promotion, their peer groups also shrink. At the top levels, leaders are often completely without peers or direct management overseeing their actions. In these situations, leaders may find they have few, if any, individuals to whom they are accountable. This is a dangerous place—lots of power but little accountability. In these situations, unhealthy pride can grow unchecked.

As you start your career and grow in leadership, you should purpose to have people in your life who you have given permission to keep you accountable. This role is commonly held by a mentor. Mentors are not just for early-career leaders. History is loaded with examples of powerful, senior leaders who had mentors even after reaching a career pinnacle. Satya Nadella was mentored by Bill Gates after taking the reins at Microsoft. Indra

Nooyi famously relied on the legendary General Electric CEO Jack Welch as her mentor after taking the CEO role at PepsiCo. Even US presidents like Abraham Lincoln, Franklin D. Roosevelt, and Barack Obama have discussed mentors they kept close after reaching the White House.

In most cases, you will need to ask the mentor to agree to formalize the mentor-mentee relationship. There is something about framing the relationship in the mentor-mentee context that confirms the authority and permission you are giving the mentor. Without this context, the relationship might more closely resemble a friendship or acquaintance. Friends and acquaintances do not sign up for the responsibility of helping guide your career and life choices like a mentor does. When the mentor-mentee relationship is agreed upon, the mentor says, "I offer you my perspective and experience so you can make better decisions." In contrast, the mentee says, "I give you permission to call out my mistakes and misunderstandings and am counting on you to help me avoid pitfalls that you see in my journey." This is much different than a friend or acquaintance relationship.

The power in the mentor-mentee relationship is the permission and authority the mentee gives to the mentor. Mentors have permission to speak truth to you about what you do well and where you can improve. The best mentors want the best for you and want to see you succeed, and they are willing to point out areas in your life where you have an inflated view of your value.

Earlier in my career, I had a mentor who helped me tremendously over the six years of our relationship. He acted as a sounding board when I needed to discuss complex situations. He offered advice when I was dealing with challenging decisions. In every case, he told me what I needed to hear rather than what I wanted to hear. Some of his feedback was difficult to hear and harder to accept. Oftentimes I found I was disappointed when he provided feedback that highlighted flaws in my thinking or actions. This is how mentors provide accountability and protection from unhealthy pride. Mentors can keep you grounded as you grow in power and influence by speaking the truth, especially hard truths highlighting areas where you need to improve.

The mentor-mentee relationship requires the mentee to trust and value the mentor's point of view. It is not a magic relationship. Even well-meaning mentees can refuse to listen to the mentor's point of view and lose the protection that point of view provides.

Back to my mentor, whom I had for many years. My mentor was a serial CEO of public US companies. He was a successful man of high character. He cared about me as a person and a leader. He was among the best allies I have ever had in my career journey. So naturally, when I presented him with one of the most important decisions in my young career, I completely ignored his advice.

I was ready to move on from my current role. I had been in my role as vice president for more than four years. It was an excellent role at an excellent company. I liked my boss and loved my team. There was nothing wrong with my role; I just felt it was time to move on. I had long had a goal of being a CIO at a public company. While I really liked the work I was doing, I felt that continuing to work as a vice president at my current organization was not getting me any closer to my goal of being a CIO at a public company. I had discussions about my desire to be a public company CIO with my mentor, who was supportive. He didn't think it was vital that I move on at that time, but he understood the premise and said a move could be helpful—if it was the right move.

I began looking for opportunities. I knew I needed more experience before I had any chance of being considered for a public CIO role, so I looked for different jobs. I looked for jobs in areas where I didn't have much experience. My premise was that I should round out my experience and prop up areas in my profile that might be seen as weak. I looked for jobs that would set me apart from all of the other CIO candidates in the future.

Eventually, I received an offer for a senior vice president role at a start-up in a field in which I had no experience. Moreover, the role was not in technology, but in customer support and customer success organization. I was certain this was the role I was looking for. After all, how much more well-rounded could I be than if I were a technology leader with customer success and sales experience? I knew it would be challenging, but I was up for it.

I shared the opportunity with my mentor and asked what he thought about the role as the next step for me. He congratulated me and told me he didn't think it was the right job. He was clear and specific about why he thought it was a bad fit. He told me what he thought my strengths were and what type of environment I thrived in. My mentor explained why elements of the new role would be challenging for me and which elements I likely would not enjoy. His focus was not on the fact that the role was outside technology. He did not voice concerns about my ability to lead a customer success organization or deal with sales. His concerns were around the size of the company and its early start-up stage.

I took the job despite his concerns. He congratulated me and helped me negotiate a good compensation package even though I did not follow his advice. He did not reiterate his objections or condemn me for not following his advice. He was an excellent mentor. But you guessed it—he was right. I worked at the start-up for a couple of years. I did not enjoy the job all that much. It might have helped round out my experience, and it looked good on my profile, but it was not a good fit. Everything my mentor warned me about was true. He read my strengths perfectly and accurately predicted the poor fit.

In retrospect, I realized why I took the job despite his assessment and recommendation. It was pride. I was so excited that a company was hiring me for my leadership skills alone. This company did not care about my technology skillset. They wanted me as a leader. That was important to me. I told myself that this company understood me like no other company had before. I told myself I finally had an opportunity to work for a company that recognized my leadership ability. I had always believed that my leadership approach was my most valuable trait, and finally, a company showed me they believed the same. It was pride.

My pride got in the way of the authority I had given my mentor. I told myself that I still wanted to hear his point of view. But what I really wanted was for him to see *my* point of view. I wanted him to be as proud of my ability to translate my leadership skills to a non-technology role as I was. When he opted to give me his honest opinion instead, I ignored his counsel and sided with my pride.

Fortunately, the cost of my prideful decision was not unbearable. I didn't enjoy my job, and it didn't help me grow as a leader, but overall it could have been worse. The company was not a good fit for me for all the reasons my mentor warned me about. If I had followed his advice, I have no doubt I would have found a better-fitting role eventually. I got lucky—but it could have been much more difficult. And all because I didn't truly grant my mentor the authority to speak the truth to me, despite claiming I had.

Finding the Right Mentor

The nature of a mentor-mentee relationship all but demands that the mentor comes from your personal network. You will be giving tremendous authority to your mentor. Granting this authority where deep trust is not already present is a tall order—perhaps too tall of an order.

Start by considering people in your network who have already walked the career path you hope to traverse. Look for experienced, successful people who you know and, more importantly, who know you well. The right mentor should see your face when they read your name. They should know you personally rather than just in an "I have seen his name in an organizational chart" sort of way.

Consider what aspects of your career growth you are most concerned about or unclear about. Are you trying to find your way into an extremely niche field where the path of access is hard to define? If you are, you need to find someone who is well-established in that niche field. Are you in a more traditional field but want to focus on nonprofits? It might be best to focus your mentor search on folks with deep non-profit experience. Do you want to grow your leadership career with integrity? If so, you must find a mentor who shares your commitment to leading the right way and avoiding integrity-impacting decisions.

Their journey does not have to be identical to yours. My mentor was a CEO when my goal was to become a CIO. My mentor was highly technically competent, but his background was in finance and accounting, not technology. Nevertheless, it was a great fit. He had a tremendously successful career in big roles while maintaining his character and integrity.

WHY YOU MAY ALSO NEED A COACH

Mentors can be highly effective at helping a growing leader navigate their career trajectory. The right mentor has "been there, done that" and can help their mentee anticipate challenges and opportunities that will arise throughout their career. Their experience in the specific domain of the mentee's career provides tremendous value. However, it is important to remember that while most mentors are experts in a specific field, domain, or approach, they are not experts in giving advice, helping leaders navigate challenges, or taking advantage of opportunities. Mentors can share, from their experience, things that worked for them and things that did not work for them. Their toolbox is full of principles that have been formulated by personal experience. Rarely, however, is their toolbox loaded with professional guidance training or structured approaches to providing advice. The mentor, as a practicing domain expert, can share their story but cannot always be counted on to share unbiased observations and objective analysis.

For that, we need to consider the professional, career, or executive coach. Career coaches are paid professionals who are engaged to act as an experienced, trained sounding board and guide. A professional coach can be effective at helping keep you accountable as you grow your career. Selecting a coach who can articulate the value of service, responsibility, teamwork, and collaboration is important.

Many coaches operate by encouraging self-reflection and discovery—helping their clients find their own answers to the questions they are dealing with. If you are candid about your desire to grow your career without taking unethical shortcuts, the right coach can help you realize the things you are most concerned about and develop strategies to deal with them. As a trusted advisor, a coach can provide honest and constructive feedback that a leader might not hear from others. This unbiased perspective helps the leader identify blind spots and areas for improvement.

For the coach to have maximum impact, you must do your part in the engagement.

- **Open to feedback:** You need to be willing and eager to hear the coach's feedback, especially when it is challenging.
- **Self-reflection:** The coach will guide you through times of self-reflection and examination. You must be an enthusiastic participant. If you do not join the coach in examining your behaviors, motivations, and tendencies, the coach will have little material to work with.
- **Bias for action:** When you hear and understand any identified challenges or blind spots, you must be motivated to improve the challenge and correct the blind spot. Hearing the issues is only helpful if it motivates you to establish a plan for solving them.

Pairing a professional coach and a mentor is a recipe for maximum accountability. The mentor acts as your wise, time-tested compatriot who can help you understand the career journey you are on. The coach can help you navigate that journey with objective, personalized insight and action plans based on your personal experience, goals, and challenges. Together, they can help the willing leader identify triggers for unhealthy pride before it hinders your ethical advancement.

It is worth noting, while mentors are commonly unpaid roles—they tend to dedicate their time due to the relationship formed with you over the years—coaches are typically paid for their services. Professional and career coaches can be pricey. Engaging a coach is an investment in your career and professional effectiveness. It should be considered in the same way you would consider pursuing an advanced degree. Both have a cost and a potential benefit to your future. Weigh the pros and cons and consider if the expense of a coach makes sense in your current season. While you can be successful without a coach, the expense of a good coach has a great return on investment in most cases.

COACHES	MENTORS
Skill-focused development	Holistic personal growth
Objective feedback	Life and career counsel
Guided self-discovery	Experience-based advice
Time-bound relationship	Long-term relationship
Structured, scheduled sessions	Flexible, informal meetings
Typically paid role	Unpaid guidance
Limited personal history	Deep personal connection
Specialized expertise	Invested in your success

HOW SELF-AWARENESS CAN SAVE YOUR JOB

When a person is self-aware, it means they have a clear understanding of what they do well and where they struggle. Being self-aware means knowing you are not an expert at everything and recognizing you have weaknesses. Unhealthy pride can be avoided by acknowledging and accounting for your weaknesses. The self-aware leader will take steps to recognize and understand their weaknesses, not ignore or hide them.

On the first day of my first good job in technology, I met my new manager's director. The director had not been involved in my interview process. In fact, there wasn't really much of an interview process. My best friend from high school, a guy who was such a close friend that we were in each other's wedding parties, was the hiring manager. My friend, also known as "my new boss," essentially hired me because he knew me and I was interested in the job. I had some relevant experience, but likely not enough to be considered a good candidate, let alone actually get hired for the role.

Nevertheless, on my first day I was in the tech room with all my new coworkers, waiting for my first assignment, when the director walked into the room. I was meeting all of my new coworkers that morning, so I assumed meeting the director would be the same. I said, "Nice to meet you. I am happy to be starting here. I am very excited about the opportunity." You know, first-day pleasantries. The foundation for future relationships. What I didn't expect was for the director, in a room full of my new peers and my new manager, to say, "I didn't get a chance to interview you, so let's do that now."

He then proceeded to ask me to describe my experience, what I thought my strengths were, and where my experience might be lacking. I started out well. I talked about areas where my experience might be lacking. I was humble. I talked about my ability to get up to speed quickly and highlighted that being coachable was one of my strengths. The director seemed engaged and nodded his head a lot but said little. He then asked me a follow-up question, and my strong start stopped. I actually said, "Well, my knowledge and experience in that area is pretty complete." I actually said that. Pro tip—never say that. Ever. Especially not in a job interview. Be confident, but never say your knowledge and experience is "complete."

That got the director's attention. He seemed to pause—almost like a glitch. He also couldn't believe this rookie would make such a statement, claiming "pretty complete" knowledge and experience of a technical practice. He nodded slowly and asked a second, more specific follow-up question. His second follow-up question would likely have required someone truly experienced in the area to answer the question completely with a lengthy, complex response. However, since my experience fell far short of "pretty complete," my answer was more of a rambling mess than a complex and complete answer. I knew I had stepped in it and oversold my knowledge and experience.

At the end of my embarrassingly inadequate answer, I said, "I am sure that answer was not close to what you were looking for. Would you mind telling me where I got it wrong?"

The director laughed a forced, insincere laugh and declared the impromptu interview complete. He left the room and called my friend...I mean, my manager, out of the room with him. My friend told me later that the director was ready to end my short employment at the company after that interview. He said the only thing that saved me was my humility in admitting my mistake at the end of my final answer, and doing so in front of the other engineers. The director said, "If not for being humble enough to admit he didn't really know the answer, he would have been gone."

This little nugget from early in my career is a perfect example of pride and boasting outstripping self-awareness and good judgment. I hadn't taken the time to examine my talents and strengths, so pride and posturing filled the gap when pressed.

Each one of us has strengths and weaknesses. We each have things we do well and areas where we struggle.

Perhaps the struggle is due to a lack of training or experience—these struggles can often be overcome with focus and time. But perhaps the struggles come from a lack of desire, passion, or motivation. Try as you might, you just cannot muster enough interest to become good at accounting or painting walls. In these cases, your ability to do accounting or paint walls may always fall short of a strength. And that is okay. But it is only okay if you allow yourself to be aware of these areas.

Self-aware leaders acknowledge their challenges and strive to surround themselves with people who exhibit strength in areas where the leader is weak. They know that each team member brings their strengths and weaknesses. Self-aware leaders know the team is stronger than the individual. They know that "we > me." Understanding and optimizing "we > me" is a powerful foundation for the integrity edge.

INVITING FEEDBACK AND HOW TO RECEIVE IT

Sometimes it can be difficult to identify and acknowledge the areas that challenge you. Or, I should say, it can be difficult for *you* to identify and acknowledge the areas that challenge you. People who know you well will likely rattle off a list of your challenges before you finish reading this paragraph. Your strengths and weaknesses are almost certainly more obvious to your closest friends and coworkers than to you. The view others have may not be perfect. Some things may remain unclear, or you might fake them well enough to delude some of your closest friends. But you will not fool them all.

Seek feedback from your peers, mentors, and coaches. Give these people explicit permission to help you identify your limitations. When they trust you enough to provide this feedback, accept it as the gift it is. Refrain from challenging or disputing their point of view. You asked them, they told you. That was the agreement. If they are willing to take the risk of telling you what they think you struggle with, accept their point of view and thank them.

Take some time by yourself to consider the feedback you have received. Does the feedback ring true to you? Can you see what they were talking about? Can you see the actions or inactions that made your friends see this area as a weakness? Perhaps you could take some time to brainstorm about their feedback, such as journaling about your thoughts on their opinions. Taking time to consider this feedback allows you to reflect and course-correct, fostering a more open and honest communication dynamic.

THE TEAMWORK EASY BUTTON

You are doing what you can to be self-aware. You have asked your peers, mentors, and coaches for insight into your strengths and weaknesses. You have taken the time to consider how your strengths and weaknesses show up.

If you want to maximize the impact of these actions on your battle against unhealthy pride, add sincere vulnerability.

Share what you know about your strengths and weaknesses with your team. Tell them you added them to the team specifically because they are strong where you are weak. Be specific about their strengths that compensate for your weaknesses. Let them know you realize your challenges and invite them to lean into those areas and help you.

Model a humble approach to self-awareness that your team can learn from and emulate. A vulnerable leader sets a powerful example for the team. It normalizes open communication and encourages team members to be vulnerable with each other, fostering a more supportive and understanding work environment. A team built in this manner is predisposed to collaboration and teamwork. It is as close to a teamwork Easy Button as you are likely to find in this life.

SUMMARY

The pride stumbling block can disproportionately impact your ability to grow a career in compassionate, high-character leadership. Unhealthy pride impacts so many aspects of your growth that it can single-handedly derail your attempts at ethical advancement.

But the path to avoiding unhealthy pride is clear and attainable:

- Remember you didn't get here alone. Remember all the people who played a role in your successful journey.
- Meet the other stars in your organization that make the entire thing work. How well would you be doing if not for them doing their parts?
- Serve others. When you focus on serving rather than being served, unhealthy pride has difficulty getting your attention.
- Focus on your people, listen to their wants and needs, and take action where possible. When you focus on your team members, you block unhealthy pride.

- Establish a habit for robust recognition. Find the people who are doing great things and champion their behaviors.
- Find a mentor and/or a coach. They can provide the antidote to unhealthy pride.
- Strive to be self-aware and vulnerable. Surround yourself with people who excel at things that challenge you. Tell your team members about your challenges and their role in helping you in these areas.

3

THE SELFISHNESS OF FEAR
Why Courageous Leaders Win in the Long Run

"Fear is a reaction. Courage is a decision."
—WINSTON CHURCHILL

I SURE LOVE A GOOD SUPERHERO STORY. Who doesn't like it when the good guys use incredible powers to save and protect the innocent? It is literally the stuff of legends and storybooks. I especially like the stories that show the hero dealing with fear before the climactic showdown with the evil, white-cat-petting supervillain. Sure, our hero can fly and lift cars and stuff...but even heroes have fear sometimes.

What makes them our heroes is the flying and car-lifting, the serving and protecting the innocent, but it is also their action in the face of fear. Superheroes wouldn't be so super if they didn't have the courage to overcome their fear. Courage is the key to avoiding the fear stumbling block.

Fear is a normal, healthy human response. Fear is an emotion and a primal human reaction designed to keep humans safe from danger. But fear also has a cognitive element. It is an emotion, but it is interpreted by our thoughts, understanding, and experiences. The emotional "fight or flight" fear response is informed by our cognitive processes. The things we see and hear, the things we have experienced in the past, and our analysis of the circumstances all influence our response to fear.

Leaders experience fear all the time. It is impossible to take a leadership journey without running into fear frequently. I am not talking about the "oh my, that is a mighty large spider" fear. I am talking about the fear leaders experience regarding the possible impact of their decisions and the impact of the decisions they avoid. I am talking about the fear that some leaders have about losing their jobs. I am talking about the fear leaders have regarding loss of power, influence, or compensation.

Fear can cloud a leader's judgment and prompt them to prioritize self-preservation over ethical decisions. What does self-preservation-motivated leadership look like? It takes many forms. Leaders might begin micromanaging their staff or attempting to control the actions and responses of their team members. Leaders may start working in secrecy or isolation, and distrust their teams. They may begin cutting corners and making misleading or even deceptive statements and claims. Leaders who succumb to the fear of losing power, influence, or compensation will sacrifice team members to keep their fear from being realized.

We have likely all seen this behavior in action: the executive who, after missing the annual sales numbers, fired the global sales leader while stating they were at fault for missing the goal; or the leader who used her predecessor as a scapegoat for any bad results. These are not the actions of an ethical leader.

While fear is unavoidable in the leadership journey, you can prepare yourself to respond to fear properly. You can prepare yourself to respond in a way that agrees with your stated goals of growing your leadership career ethically. Our goal is to arm ourselves with tools that help us have courage in the face of fear. Courage doesn't make the fear go away. Courage is doing the right thing despite the fear.

The key to preparing yourself to make good decisions when wrestling with fear is cultivating powerful, positive emotions and motivations you can feed on instead of making fear-motivated decisions. Arming yourself with these positive emotions and motivations will help you have the courage to make ethical decisions.

Courage is doing the right thing despite the fear.

In this section, I discuss strategies for building three powerful emotions and motivations that can act as a counterbalance to fear and empower you to make high-character choices. The three courage-creating motivators are:

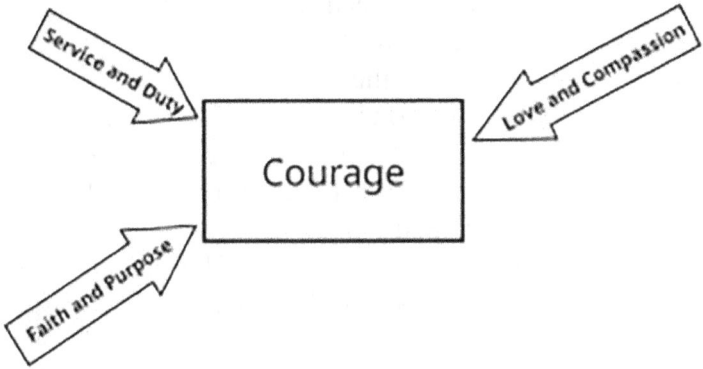

1. Faith and purpose
2. Service and duty
3. Love and compassion

As you build these motivators, fear may still visit you occasionally, but it will not be alone. You will have these motivators as tools to combat the fear, act with courage, and continue to make principled decisions.

Keep in mind that these motivators are not like light switches that you never think about until you need them, and then, voila, flip a switch and there is light. These motivators do not work like that. If you never prepare them, when you flip the switch, there will not be light. These motivators must be invested in ahead of time. Deposit time, attention, and intention when you are not experiencing fear, and these motivators will be the light you need when the fear comes.

FAITH, PURPOSE, AND CONVICTION

Strong faith and conviction in a higher purpose or guiding principles can give you the courage to act ethically, even in the face of fear. This can mean having courage because of a religious or spiritual conviction. Many people are deeply motivated by faith in a higher power. But it can also mean having courage because you have committed yourself to being an ethical leader, which has become a conviction. To develop this conviction, we must focus on a principle Simon Sinek made popular: "Start with why."

In his 2009 book, *Start with Why: How Great Leaders Inspire Everyone to Take Action*, Simon Sinek argues that great leaders inspire people by starting with "why," which is their purpose, cause, or belief. Once convicted of this purpose or belief, they articulate "how" they plan to achieve that purpose and, finally, "what" products or services they offer. By defining their purpose first, great leaders give direction and meaning to their actions and clearly understand their guiding principles.[ix]

We can build a powerful, courage-building motivational tool in the same manner. By starting with "why," we create a powerful anchor that we can use to challenge any knee-jerk desire to respond to fear unethically. How do we come to better understand our "why?" How do we develop a conviction in our purpose and beliefs to the point where it becomes an effective antidote to fear-based decision-making?

We must spend time on deeply understanding our purpose and beliefs. A superficial, greeting-card-style statement about our beliefs isn't going to get it done. We need a deep understanding. We need to make deposits into these purposes and beliefs so the balance will be high when we come face-to-face with fear and need to act.

My oldest granddaughter, Kayden, is a dancer. Although she has been dancing for less than five years at the time of writing this book, her passion for dance and commitment to training and getting better are awe-inspiring. Within her first year of dancing, she decided she wanted to have a career as a dancer, and she is training like she means it.

A couple of years ago, when she had only been dancing for two or three years, she got an amazing opportunity to train for a solo competition with the director of her dance studio. It bears mentioning that this director had never coached or choreographed a solo dance for anyone other than her own children. Nevertheless, the director saw something in my granddaughter and offered to choreograph a solo and coach her for a scheduled competition. Although Kayden was nervous about the opportunity, she said yes and immediately started training with the director. I mean serious training—many hours a day, many days each week. For months.

Now, teenage girls being teenage girls, the ridicule Kayden got from the other dancers at the studio was, at times, nearly unbearable. The other dancers said all kinds of hateful things.

"Why do you get to be coached by the director? You are not nearly as good of a dancer as I am."

"You shouldn't be doing a solo with the director. You have only been dancing for three years."

"You are going to embarrass yourself and the director because you are not as good as her son is."

And far worse. They said all of the things we would hate to hear.

This is how it went for months leading up to the competition: hardcore training and never-ending heckling from her fellow dancers. It created a tremendous amount of stress on Kayden. She is a confident dancer, but even the most confident among us wrestles with self-doubt and uncertainty. Kayden was no different. Finally, the competition weekend arrived.

My granddaughter was thirteen at the time of the competition. Thirteen was a very important age for this particular competition.

The age groups were:

- 12 and under
- 13 and over (to 19)

This was her first competition dancing against girls with as many as ten or more years of experience and, in some cases, were heading off to college in the fall. Pause. Think about that. Thirteen years old versus nineteen years old. Three years of experience versus ten years of experience.

Friday and Saturday went well. Her company (group) dances were great. Her duet on Sunday morning went very well. She and her partner won 3rd place in the thirteen-year-plus age group.

Her solo was scheduled for Sunday afternoon. She completely psyched herself out about it. Her solo was the second to the last dance of the competition, and there were more than eighty dancers in her age group. Kayden had to watch every other dancer—older and more experienced than she was—while waiting for her slot. The weight of the situation had finally gotten to be too much. Oh, wait. I forgot to mention that the director of her studio was the emcee of this particular dance competition. Although the judges were independent and unaffiliated with any of the competitors, her coach, choreographer, and studio director was the emcee. Kayden's concern that she would not represent her coach well was amplified by the fact that her coach was the most visible adult at the competition—on the microphone after each dance and on the stage after each group. I am sure Kayden imagined her coach taking the stage in her emcee responsibilities immediately after everyone watched her mess up.

To recap:

- The director had only coached or choreographed her children's solos in the past.
- The other dancers in the studio didn't think my granddaughter was worthy.
- She had to watch eighty older and more experienced dancers' solos.
- She was the second to the last dancer in the entire competition.
- Her coach and choreographer was the emcee of the competition.

There, that more properly sets the stage.

All of this got in her head. Nervous does not begin to describe her state of mind. There were tears—lots of tears. She decided she simply could not do the dance. She wasn't good enough—the girls were right. She was going to fail.

She was going to embarrass herself and her coach. It was all too much.

Eventually my wife and I had to take our seats and wait as dance #354 became #355, then #356. All the while, we didn't know if she would be on stage when #360 was called. I would have given it even odds, but I wasn't sure.

Well, when #360 was called, my little lady took the stage, and SHE KILLED IT! She mustered courage like I have rarely seen. She would likely have won the competition if the Hallmark Channel had played this story, but this is real life. In real life, this scared thirteen-year-old with failing self-confidence placed fourth out of eighty-two dancers and received one of the three "Judge's Choice" awards.

She took the stage despite the overwhelming fear of failure. I asked her later, "You were so scared. Terrified. Why did you take the stage and dance if you were so scared?"

She told me, "I wanted to prove myself wrong. Not prove others wrong, but prove it to myself. I kept telling myself I wasn't good enough, but I didn't believe that. I knew that God would help me. I knew that He could help me, and I wanted to prove it to myself. Also, the dance was about anxiety and getting through anxious times. I knew the message could help others who struggle like I was. Like I do. Besides, I am going to be a dancer, and dancers dance."

This scared thirteen-year-old came to the battle with fear, but was armed with faith and convicted by her purpose. She had been establishing these motivations for years. She had continued to press into them throughout the year as she trained and dealt with rude remarks at the dance studio. She took time to understand what was most important to her—what her foundation was. When confronted with the crippling fear of failure, she pressed into the deposits she had made in her faith and purpose. She had faith that God would help her. She wanted to dance a dance that would help anxious girls like her. She was laser-focused on being a dancer. These motivations were enough for her to act contrary to her fear.

How can we strengthen our faith and purpose so they will provide an effective weapon against fear-based decision-making? We can learn a lot from a thirteen-year-old dancer. What exercises and approaches can we use to establish a conviction for a specific purpose or belief?

Self-Reflection

Get ready. You need to do deep, personal, and deeply introspective work. Faith, purpose, and conviction are personal motivators that come from deep within each of us. To establish a deeper understanding of your personal values and motivations, you'll need to set aside some time to purposefully discover what is important to you, what motivates you, and why. You will need to do some dreaming. What does your future look like? What do you want to accomplish in your life, and why?

Take some time to brainstorm what is important to you. What do you value in your life? What do you value about your most important relationships? Literally, brainstorm about these things and prepare a list. Prioritize the list. Write down the product of your brainstorming and consider why each value is important to you. Can you identify your top three values? Can you determine what you value most in life?

Take some time to brainstorm what motivates you. Think about what you hope to accomplish in your life—in all of your life. For the sake of this exercise, do not separate work from family or personal life. Combine them. When your days are done, what do you hope you have accomplished? Spend some serious time thinking about that. But don't just think about it. Write down what you come up with. Something about writing things down forces us to dig a little deeper. Our mind may let us stop with an incomplete understanding of a thing and be satisfied by some progress. But if you are anything like me, incomplete thoughts and sentences on a page scream at me to be completed. Writing things down often helps us think about things more thoroughly.

If you have done this exercise correctly and exhaustively, you will have a well-thought-out list of values and motivations. You will have examined why each of these things is important to you. You should have noticed patterns between your values, motivations, and what you hope to accomplish. Hint: most people want to involve themselves in activities they value and that motivate them. And most people want to be someone they could be motivated by and find value in. Outside of legitimate medical and mental conditions, most people want to be someone they are happy to see in the mirror. Effective self-reflection can help establish and articulate your faith and purpose.

External Considerations

Beyond self-reflection, there is much to be learned about our faith and purpose from other sources. Consider three additional sources for insights into building and establishing a conviction for your faith and purpose: personal experiences, role models, and trusted opinions.

Your personal experiences can tell you a lot about your faith and purpose. Consider your many successes and failures over the years. What experiences spark a sense of fulfillment? Which successes are you most proud of? Can you articulate why the accomplishment fills you with a sense of pride? What specific accomplishments brought you the most satisfaction and joy? Why?

What have you done in the past that embarrasses you? What about the experience embarrasses you? I am not talking about when you went to a podium to speak and learned later that your fly was unzipped. I am talking about someone getting hurt when you didn't tell the truth about something. I am talking about when you wanted to help someone in a tough situation but didn't because you feared how it would make you look. Think about these blemishes on your record and consider why they make you feel bad.

Our own experiences can tell us much about our values and motivations. They can shed tremendous light on our faith and purpose. When our actions make us feel happy and joyful and give us a sense of accomplishment, we are likely on the path of purpose. When our actions make us feel cheap, dirty, unworthy, or cowardly, we are likely acting contrary to our faith or purpose. Take note of how your experiences align with common themes.

We can also glean insight into our faith and purpose from other people. Consider your role models and the people you trust the most in your life. What do you admire about your role models? Can you identify their purpose? What is their "why"? Why do you consider them role models? What is it about their behavior or character that you find appealing?

Do you know your role model enough to ask them about their faith and purpose? If you do, ask them. Do it now. Schedule a conversation with your role model and ask them about their faith and purpose. Ask them if they can articulate why they do what they do. What makes them tick? You admire them—perhaps there is something you can learn about your purpose from an explanation of theirs. This is not to suggest that you try to emulate your role model's purpose and adopt it as your own. This is just to suggest that you admire them because you see something appealing in what they do or how they do it. Examine that. Find out what you can learn about yourself from them.

Finally, don't be afraid to ask someone who knows you well and who you trust implicitly to tell you what they think your purpose is. Ask them what they believe you value most and what motivates you. We each tell ourselves stories about who we are. Sometimes the stories we tell ourselves are fiction, but fictions told so well we do not recognize they are false. At times like this, it can be truly eye-opening to get someone else's point of view.

Now, one word of caution. When you ask your closest, trusted loved one this question, don't attack them when they answer. Resist the urge to correct them. Take their feedback as a gift. Glean whatever value you can from it. It might not completely align with the story you have been telling yourself, but see if there is any truth in their point of view. Can you see why they believe what they do? Can you understand their explanation of your most strongly held convictions? What does that do to help you understand your faith and purpose?

The exercises that build our faith and convict us of our purposes are not one-time activities. These must be life-long pursuits. Faith and purpose are like muscles. Nobody ever got six-pack abdominal muscles from doing one crunch. Your faith and purpose will not be the fear-beating tools we need from a single brainstorming session or meditation. Prioritize understanding and building on your faith and purpose, and it will be a strong defense against regrettable, fear-based decision-making.

Prioritize understanding and building on your faith and purpose, and it will be a strong defense against regrettable, fear-based decision-making.

SERVICE AND DUTY

A strong sense of service and duty can help create the courage to act even when it might be personally risky. It's similar to the courage the firefighter summons as they run into the burning building to save someone. It is like the courage a soldier musters when they stand shoulder to shoulder with a fellow soldier in a pitched battle. It is how the police officer can run into a high school when there is an active shooter.

In each of these examples, the individual summoning the courage to act does so because they have a responsibility to act—a duty. They are protecting and serving someone who needs them to act. In many cases, they find the courage to act because they feel an intense obligation to the people who are counting on them.

A leader summoning the courage to act ethically, putting themself at personal risk of retribution or censure, is similar to what the soldier and police officer had to summon to put themselves in physical harm's way. I am not suggesting that a leader standing up to her boss when asked to do something unethical takes the same courage as hunting down an active school shooter or walking into a burning building. The stakes are not equal. It is career versus life. I get the difference. The point is that the process of overcoming their fear enough to take action is the same. A leader with a strong sense of service and duty to the people in their charge, the mission of their team, and their obligation to act ethically might have sufficient motivation to take the right actions that could put their career in harm's way.

Given that this book aims to help leaders who desire to grow their careers with integrity, we must review methods for overcoming the fear that causes many would-be-leaders-of-character to stumble and make decisions contrary to their desire to act ethically. Developing a strong sense of service to your team and mission, and deepening your sense of duty to act ethically, will help you when you face these burning-building moments in your career.

A few years ago, a leader I have known for more than a decade showed what it looks like when service and duty overrule fear of negative personal impact. Let's call the leader Scott. Scott made a mistake that emotionally hurt one of the leaders on his team. It was a complete accident, and Scott immediately felt awful. Now, Scott was the boss. He could have bottled up his awful feelings, stood high on his title, and left the subordinate leader to deal with his hurt feelings. But that is not what Scott did.

What did he do? Scott reached out to the person hurt by his mistake, acknowledged the mistake, apologized for the carelessness that caused the accident, and did what he could to lighten the emotional toll. If this is all he did, it is hardly worth mentioning in this book. Nothing about apologizing to the person he hurt is going to cause him a personal loss. So what else did he do?

He then reached out individually to the three peers of the person hurt by the mistake who happened to witness the situation. Scott apologized to each of the peers for what they witnessed, for the mistake, and for any impact it had on them. He didn't try to explain why he made the mistake—he just apologized for the error and asked if he could answer any questions the situation might have created. But he wasn't finished.

Scott then contacted human resources to let them know what happened. He wanted human resources to be aware in case there was anything they could do to help the person who was impacted. He fully owned the mistake and its impact. He fully acknowledged that his carelessness caused the incident and that he had hurt one of his team members. This final step, reaching out to human resources, could have resulted in several negative consequences. Scott's burden for serving his team members and his absolute commitment to acting with integrity allowed him to enlist assistance from human resources even though doing so might have cost him.

What was Scott thinking? He was under no obligation to contact human resources. He had made a mistake, but mistakes happen. There is no need to make more of this than what it is. The person will be fine...eventually. But when he went to HR, there was no telling what might happen. When human resources got involved, his position at the company could have been compromised.

However, for Scott the threat of negative impact on his job was insufficient to prevent him from serving his team members. He knew they needed something from him and, despite the possible personal cost, he felt a conviction to act on their behalf. He felt stronger about the need to help his team than he felt about the need to protect himself. That is what courage born of a strong sense of service and duty looks like.

How did Scott develop this strong sense of service and duty? Knowing Scott as I do, I can say with certainty that he had been building that sense of service and duty long before I met him. Looking back, there are a few things Scott did routinely that likely helped him cultivate and maintain his focus on serving his team members.

Let's focus on three activities that helped Scott develop his sense of service. When performed over time, these activities will help develop the motivating power of service and duty and allow them to influence courageous action in the face of fear.

1. Focusing on the company mission, the team mission, and a personal mission
2. Communicating with the team members
3. Building relationships with the team members

To help explain why these activities can help build a powerful sense of service and duty, consider the following story of a below-average baseball player.

When I was growing up, my family moved a lot. My father was in the Army, so we moved every three or four years throughout my entire childhood. Our final move was between my freshman and sophomore year in high school. We lived in West Germany for a few years and moved to Oklahoma during the summer. While my father was stationed at Fort Sill, just north of the small military town of Lawton, Oklahoma, my family lived in the tiny rural town of Geronimo, Oklahoma. But as circumstance would have it, we didn't move directly from Germany to Geronimo. There were several months of transitional housing and temporary schooling. Because of this transitionary period, I didn't get to Geronimo High School, home of the mighty Blue Jays, until the winter of my sophomore year.

I don't recall exactly when we arrived in Geronimo, but I had not been in the school for more than a few weeks when baseball season started. It bears mentioning that baseball was not my true love. American football has always had my heart. Unfortunately, Geronimo High School did not have a football team. The town and high school were simply too small to support a football team. So baseball became my sport. The first day of baseball practice was in January or February.

Let's recap. I was a moody teenager. I had just moved away from my friends in Germany to rural Oklahoma. I didn't know anybody at the new school. And I was settling for playing baseball because this tiny school didn't even have a football team.

I honestly don't remember the first baseball practice. Given the background I just described, I suspect I did enough that I didn't stand out as a slacker in practice. But I cannot imagine that I left it all on the field. At that point in my run as a below-average baseball player on the Geronimo Blue Jays, I was only playing for myself and the enjoyment of the game. I was not playing or practicing for my team. How could I? I didn't know my team. No part of my identity was connected with Geronimo, Oklahoma, or the mighty Blue Jays. I had not established these motivators yet. So on my first day of practice, my only motivations were to not get yelled at by the coaches and to try to have fun.

All of this changed with time. Eventually, I forged friendships with my teammates. I got to know them, and they got to know me. Eventually, the Geronimo Blue Jays became important to me because of what the school and team meant to my classmates. As the year progressed and my sophomore year became my junior and then senior years, my motivations changed. I didn't lose the motivations I had. I still wanted to keep from being yelled at by the coaches and I still wanted to have fun. But now, I was motivated to not let my teammates down. I was motivated to get better to win games for the Blue Jays. As my affiliation and understanding of the town, the team, and the teammates grew, the motivation to serve them grew. Eventually, these motivators grew to the point of influencing my effort in practice and on game day.

The same journey happens in the workplace. As we become more aware of our workplace's activities, missions, team members, and values, they become more important to us. The increase in importance correlates with an increase in the motivational effect of our service and duty in this context. Let's look at the three activities Scott used to develop his sense of service and duty.

Personal Mission

The motivating power of service and duty comes from a personal realization of the impact you have on the lives of the people you serve and the organization you serve. Understanding the stakes in your service can help increase its ability to motivate you. To amplify the motivational power of service and duty, you need only spend time purposefully focusing on the missions you are pursuing.

You are a leader. On a team. At a company. You have a personal mission, the team you are on has a mission, and the company you work for has a mission. In each case, your work impacts whether or not those missions are accomplished. Your successes and failures impact those missions.

Your mission consists of your goals and objectives, as well as your principles and values. The goals and objectives include the things you are obligated to do at work, but they also include personal and family goals. Are you a mother or father? Do you desire to be a good parent for your children? If you do, part of your personal mission is to be present for your child and to raise your child as well as you can. Is it important to you to show compassion when you see people going through hardships or dealing with personal loss? If this is important to you, you could say that part of your mission is to be compassionate and help people who are going through difficult times.

Take time to explore the goals, objectives, principles, and values that define your mission. Schedule a meeting with yourself. Do some there-is-no-bad-answer brain-storming. Write down all the things you can think of that are important to you. Things you want to accomplish. Behaviors you want to cultivate. Traits you hope to demonstrate. Write them down. Take more time to refine the list. Are there tiers of traits and behaviors? Are some more important to you than others?

Perhaps you are thinking, "Wait, didn't we just do this?" Nope. This is not the same exercise as the introspective brainstorming we did for "faith and purpose." Think of that first exercise as focusing on "life in general," whereas this one focuses on you, your team, or your family.

You have a list of things that are important to you. Now, prioritize the list. Which of the things are most important to you? Can you place all the things you listed in order of importance? Try. Now, look at the prioritized list of objectives, traits, and behaviors. Does it look like it describes the person you want to be? Ask the person who you trust most in the world and the person who knows you best what they think of the list. Can they provide any insight into the person that your list describes?

Obviously, this is not an exercise that one completes in an afternoon. This is a deliberate, introspective exercise you perform over time. The outcome you seek is a deeper understanding of what is most important to you. What objectives, behaviors, and traits convict and constrain you? What is most important to you? How well do you understand these things? If you can cultivate a deep understanding of the things that are most important to you, you can amplify the motivating power of service and duty to those things.

The act of contemplating your personal mission and motivations will strengthen your convictions. For example, as you dwell on your desire to be a good parent, the reasons this is important to you become clearer. You become more aware of the nuances and details of the result of you being a good parent. This clarity drives conviction. If you take time to consider your personal mission—really take time—your mission will become more real, and it will sustain you when you are confronted with fear.

Team Mission, Company Mission

To supersize the motivating impact of mission, include your team and company missions in your brainstorming and contemplation sessions. Your personal mission will likely be the most motivating mission. When it comes to standing in the face of fear, the things that are most important to you are likely to have the most impact. But do not underestimate the motivating power of your team's and company's missions.

In some cases, these missions might not carry a great deal of motivating influence. I can imagine some industries that do not bring much to the being-motivated-by-the-mission game. But, in other cases, they can add a great deal. Imagine the leader of a SWAT team responding to a hostage situation. Imagine the leader of a surgical team at a children's hospital. Consider the pilot of Air Force One en route to a peace conference. In these extreme examples, it is easy to see the influence team and company missions will have on the subjects of the examples.

What fears do you suppose the SWAT team leader is better able to stand up to when she thinks of saving the hostages? What fears do you think the surgical team leader might be able to deal with when he thinks of the child they might save? Do you think the pilot can overcome some fearful situations by imagining the impact his passenger might have in the peace conference?

The same approach you use to deepen the impact of your personal mission will work with the team and company mission. It takes time, focus, and intention. If the company and team missions are not formally documented—start there. What does your company do? Who does the company impact? How do they impact them? Don't just look superficially—look deeply. Who is enriched because of the impact your company makes? How does your company improve people, communities, economies, lives, or relationships? Admittedly, some companies' missions are going to be more difficult than others. My examples were law enforcement, healthcare, and politics. If you are involved in food service, apparel, entertainment, financial services, or similar industries, the motivating mission may take longer to consider.

Let's try a more difficult example. What if you worked in food service? Let's say you are the manager of the waitstaff at a family restaurant. What about the company's mission could we focus on? Can you imagine a family that is going through some tough times coming in for dinner? Maybe they are exhausted and emotionally spent. Maybe there is marital strife. Maybe they are dealing with grief from losing a loved one recently. How much impact can your serving team have on their attitude and mental state—if even for a short time? Can you imagine the family enjoying the service at your restaurant enough that they forget their troubles for a time? Can you imagine helping the family escape their thoughts about more difficult things for an hour or so? If you can, you are on the right track. Work on scenarios in which your team's service, attention to detail, and professionalism might have a positive impact on your customers. Develop the story with nuances and details. This is how a team and company mission become more real.

Communicate with Your Team Members

The second thing Scott did that provided some of the motivation he needed to face his fear with grace is that he routinely communicated with his team members. He shared stories of the team's impact with his team members. He shared stories of the *company*'s impact with the team members. He helped them understand how their work impacted the company's work. And he helped the team understand how the company's work impacted lives.

He used small group meetings, full team meetings, and one-on-one meetings. He shared metrics that illustrated the team's positive results. He told stories about the company's impact. He solicited testimonials from customers. He talked to leaders of other company teams to understand how important his team's mission was to their success.

Scott dug deep to understand the team and company impact and found many ways to share his understanding with his team members. This served two purposes.

First, his team members were motivated by the stories. True, some employees were not motivated. Some employees were not engaged enough to be motivated. However, some employees were interested, and Scott's stories and focus on the effect they were having added to their engagement. Some employees began to see more clearly how their actions were consequential to the company's ability to achieve its goals. Some team members were even able to see how their actions impacted the lives of the company's customers.

Secondly, gathering information, stories, and testimonials continued to build up Scott's motivation. Each time he collected a story, it had a positive influence on what was driving him. Each time he talked with a colleague about his team's impact and importance to the peer's team, it had a positive influence on his motivation. Each time he told his team about the impact they were having, it had a positive influence on their desire to do good work.

Gathering, preparing, and presenting these meaningful, impactful stories developed Scott's understanding of the work he and his team were doing. These actions, coupled with his brainstorming and contemplation sessions, created a deeper understanding of his team's and his company's impact. Scott's desire—consciously or subconsciously, I am not sure—to serve those affected by his actions increased. As a result, his sense of duty and service to his role and the actions he was responsible for grew.

Spend Time Getting to Know Your Team Members

The final thing Scott did that allowed him the courage to overcome his fear and make the right decision was getting to know his team members as individuals. He made time to talk with each person. He learned about their families. He learned about their career aspirations. Scott purposefully learned more about them than just their work capabilities. He had one-on-one discussions with his team members and asked them about their hobbies and their dreams. He got to know his team members personally.

Getting to know his team members this way gave him a deeper insight into the people he served. It made them more real. When confronted with fear, he was able to muster courage based on his knowledge of the specific people he was serving. His was not courage built on a sense of service toward a generic employee. His courage was built on service to someone specific. It wasn't "I am serving my team members." It was "I am serving Sally—mother of two, avid runner, bird lover, and karaoke singer." His courage was strengthened because he developed personal knowledge and relationships with the people on his team.

Among the activities Scott used to enhance the motivating power of service and duty, this is the easiest task, but also the most easily forgotten. Spending time with your team members and getting to know them requires intentionality and a great deal of time. This can't be accomplished with a single elevator conversation. This sort of knowledge and relationship is the fruit of many conversations—some short, some long, some in person, some via email or instant message. Some of your team members will not be interested in having conversations about personal matters with you—you need to be okay with that. Others will be apprehensive at first, while others will happily talk your ear off—you need to be okay with that, too.

The keys to being effective in this endeavor are:

1. Be sincere. Your goal is to learn more about them. Ask questions and listen. Interact with the team members honestly. Do not fake interest. They will recognize it as fake, and it will sabotage your efforts.
2. Be persistent. This is not a one-time activity. Commit to reach out to the team members on a regular basis. Schedule some one-on-ones, but also send some unscheduled instant messages to see how things are going. Build your knowledge and the relationship little by little.
3. Offer insight into your personal life. Resist any urge to keep your personal life private if you are asking others to share about their families and dreams. You don't have to overshare, but you should be willing to share some personal nuggets with your team members.

4. Respect privacy. Some team members will not feel comfortable sharing personal matters with you. You must respect that and do not force them to share. Honor their privacy.

LOVE AND COMPASSION

The final category of courage-creating motivators is love and compassion. This category is tricky. To explain why it is tricky, let's consider an obvious situation where fear was overcome through the power of love.

I once heard a story about Jessica and her beautiful six-year-old daughter Alice, Jessica's only child. Jessica and Alice were on a late afternoon walk through a wooded area—beautiful weather and beautiful nature, not a care in the world. All that suddenly changed when Jessica saw a large black bear some distance from the trail and heading slowly in their direction.

Jessica was immediately gripped by cold, debilitating fear. Despite the distance between her and the bear, Jessica would swear she could see the bear's massive claws, sharp teeth, and menacing eyes. Alice, oblivious to the danger, continued skipping and singing. Her continuing joy sharply contrasted the growing dread and fear her mother felt.

Jessica's mind raced. *Stand perfectly still, and he won't see you. Run away. No, protect Alice.*

At that moment, Jessica remembered a survival tip she had read when preparing for this trip: "When you confront a bear in the wild, make yourself look as large as possible and make a lot of loud noise."

A surge of adrenaline fueled Jessica's actions. In a tone and volume she would later swear she was incapable of producing, Jessica shouted, "Alice come here. Run!

Fast! Run!" Alice was startled only momentarily before Jessica's intensity set her feet in motion. She ran to her mother as fast as she had ever run. As she got near to her mother, Jessica pointed down the trail from which they had come and, in the same commanding tone and with the same thundering volume, she yelled, "Keep running! Run, Alice! Back where we came from! I will be right behind you!"

Alice, with tears streaming and unsure of what was happening, did as she was told and ran back the way they had come. Perhaps she didn't run as fast as she started, but she did what her mother told her.

Jessica turned her attention to the bear. The yelling was having an impact. The bear was still advancing, but it had slowed. The bear seemed confused. If it were possible for the embodiment of terror to be confused, Jessica would have said it was.

She was terrified, but with adrenaline coursing through her veins and a powerful need to protect Alice, Jessica stood tall. She raised her hands over her head and even made her hands into animalistic claws. She took a few confident steps toward the bear. She continued to yell— more noise than words at this point. The bear hesitated. For a long moment, a never-ending moment, the bear stared and the mother yelled. Separated by less than thirty feet, they stared at each other. And then, as quickly as the bear appeared, it turned around and slowly walked away. Within thirty seconds, Jessica could no longer see the bear. Abruptly, she noticed she was still yelling—voice now hoarse and tears streaming down her face, menacing clawed hands lifted high, she continued to yell.

Jessica fell to her knees and stopped yelling, but she immediately thought of Alice. She jumped to her feet and turned down the path from where they had come. Alice hadn't made it very far down the path. In seconds, Jessica reached Alice and scooped her up in a giant hug.

Jessica had faced a fear greater than anything she could have imagined. When confronted with certain death, she thought clearly, acted decisively, and saved her daughter and herself. Had she been alone in the forest, Jessica was not certain she would have made the same decision. Somehow she knew that saving her daughter was the only thing that kept her thinking clearly.

It is unlikely that any of us will be called to defend our team members against an actual bear. However, the principle of responding to fear with courage is highly relevant.

How did Jessica muster the courage to literally face her fear? The answer is obvious—she loved her daughter more than she feared the bear. The love between a parent and their child is unmatched in all the world. I will not try to convince you this sort of bond is likely, or even possible, between a leader and her followers. But is it possible for love to grow in potency outside of the parent-and-child relationship?

I believe it is. And I believe the answer to how can be found in Jessica and Alice's relationship.

Acts of service between individuals will foster a deep connection over time. When we consistently consider and meet the needs of another person, we create a foundation of trust and respect. That trust and respect are the fertile ground in which a kind of love can grow.

Jessica had been considering and meeting Alice's needs and desires for over six years. As Jessica met Alice's needs and desires, Alice reciprocated and satisfied many of Jessica's needs as a mother. Jessica's service and Alice's response created an interdependence that caused their relationship to grow, and the love between them to become more potent.

A proper leader considers the needs of their team members and meets their needs. As the team members' needs are met, they become more productive and able to accomplish the team's goals and objectives. The leader serves. The team produces. Over time this relationship develops into a deep connection.

It is not the same kind of "love" as a mother has for her daughter. It is the "brotherly love" of sports teammates and childhood friends. It's the love that says, "I've got your back, and I know you've got mine, and I love you for that." This is the kind of love that is possible, even likely, when leaders lead their teams properly.

Building Relationships That Produce Love and Compassion

We have already discussed many of the actions required to produce this "brotherly love" and will cover others in more depth later in this book. To cultivate this connection with your team, you must create an environment that encourages trust (chapter 3). You must establish a routine of having one-on-one discussions with your team members (more about this in chapter 5). During these meetings, you will develop and practice active listening skills (again, chapter 5). The team members must see you caring about and serving them honestly. When these behaviors become part of your identity, the love and compassion we are discussing will follow. As you engage and serve the team, your connection to them increases.

How, then, do we ensure these behaviors become part of your identity? Well, the secret is no secret at all: consistency, availability, and follow-through.

Being *consistent* builds trust and demonstrates reliability. Consistency develops expectations. If you always respond in a certain manner, others begin to expect that response. If you consistently show up the same way—over and over—that behavior will become part of your identity. When that behavior is positive and in service to your team, the team will begin to see you as a leader who is focused on serving rather than building your empire. Consistency in behavior will make your mission believable to your team.

Being *available* ensures you are present when team members need you most. I realize you are busy. I realize you have a lot of demands on your time. Regardless, if building relationships with your team members is a priority, on just about any given day you will be able to find ten minutes for an urgent discussion. When a team member needs your insight, being available increases trust.

Imagine how you would feel if every time you reached out to your leader for assistance or advice, they were never available to help. What if every time you reached out you got a message saying, "Sorry, I am busy. I don't have time this week. Try to find some time on my calendar in the next month." That is not the sort of response that suggests this leader is someone you can count on.

What if, on the other hand, the response you got was, "I am on a call right now, but I am sure we can find some time to chat. How about I reach out to you when I get out of this meeting?" Or better yet, "I am on a call right now. Is this urgent? Do I need to step out for a few minutes, or can I reach out to you when it's over?" Being available is a key ingredient to successfully establishing meaningful relationships with your team members.

Following through on commitments is the glue of relationship building. Nothing else you do matters if the people following you do not believe what you tell them. Consider our previous example: "Can I reach out to you when this call is over?" That is only an effective response if you actually reach out to the person when the call is over. If, through consistent failure to follow through, you teach your team that you cannot be trusted to do what you say you will do, you have no hope of building deep relationships. Following through on commitments is a key ingredient to establishing meaningful relationships.

Nothing else you do matters if the people following you do not believe what you tell them.

FINAL THOUGHTS ON FEAR

Okay. We have identified a few courage-creating motivators and discussed how to build these motivators. We know it will not happen unless we consciously focus on the actions required to strengthen the motivators. But what else? What else should we know so we can have courage in the face of fear?

Two final thoughts:

- Take advantage of your fear
- Take action

What if we could use fear as a signal—a leading performance indicator of what comes next? What if we practiced recognizing the situations that typically result in fear and began acting preemptively?

A friend of mine, Chad, told me about a time early in his career when he was in a good job that wasn't the right job. I suspect you know the type of situation he was dealing with. He was in a good position—work and coworkers he liked, fair compensation, and all in a field he was passionate about—but it wasn't getting him where he wanted to be. He believed he had reached a point where he needed to make a move.

The prospect of tendering his resignation was a debilitating fear for my friend. He cared about the small company, his coworkers, and his boss, and telling his boss he was leaving was a terrifying proposition.

Chad sought his father's counsel, telling him what he liked about his role and why he needed to make a move. He explained his reluctance and fear and asked what his father thought he should do. His father asked, "What would it take for you to stay, Chad?"

This question opened Chad's eyes. He had not considered the possibility of being able to change what he didn't like about the job. He just knew the job wasn't right. Chad prepared an answer to his father's question and met with his boss. When his boss asked, "What will it take for you to stay?" Chad was prepared. Long story short, Chad stayed.

When Chad decided to resign, he recognized the fear that the decision was creating. He might not have known it was fear at the time, but he saw it as an obstacle, a source of friction for a decision he needed to make. Chad's response was to prepare. He took preemptive action because he saw the fear building. Because he took preemptive action and prepared for the encounter, much of the fear was neutralized, and Chad was able to act with courage.

What if we established a personal practice of treating the onset of fear in this manner all the time? What if, when we see signs of fear creeping in, we get aggressive in our response? What if, instead of passively hoping, we acted with courage, recognizing what was coming next and arriving at the confrontation prepared?

Like Chad, what if we examined approaching confrontation, sought counsel, and prepared for the encounter? If we start acting in this manner, fear becomes a leading indicator. Leading indicators are a bit like a glimpse into the future. They are the holy grail of planning.

If we can get to a point of recognizing fear as it is growing, we can train ourselves to take action.

Taking action can decrease the debilitating consequence of fear. Preemptive action at the trigger of fear removes some of the sting. The more you practice taking actions despite the fear, the easier these actions become. In this way, courage is like a muscle. It can be strengthened. The first time you force yourself to act in the face of fear, it may be like trying to move a mountain. But, as you continue to force yourself to act in these situations, you build a sort of muscle memory, and courageous action becomes a bit more normal, a bit easier each time. I am not saying it will ever be easy to act when fear threatens to paralyze you. But, like lifting heavy weights, the more you do it, the more weight you can handle.

SUMMARY

Fear is a stumbling block that looks different to each leader. It is unlikely you will make it through your ethical leadership journey without facing fear. Instead, you must prepare weapons and defenses to call on when the fear comes. Avoiding this stumbling block involves preparing effective positive motivators you can call on when the fear arrives.

Three courage-creating motivators:

- Faith and purpose
- Service and duty
- Love and compassion

Actions you can take to increase the effectiveness of the three motivators:

- Establish your faith and purpose: Self-Reflection
- Establish your faith and purpose: External Considerations
- What is your personal mission?
- Focus on your team's mission and your company's mission
- Communicate with your team members
- Spend time getting to know your team members
- Create relationships that produce love and compassion
- Use fear to your advantage and take action

4

AMBITION WITHOUT REGRET
How to Climb the Ladder without Losing Your Soul

"Before you are a leader, success is all about growing yourself. When you become a leader, success is all about growing others."

—JACK WELCH, *former CEO of General Electric and author of* Winning[x]

HEALTHY AMBITION is a powerful catalyst for growth and achievement. However, when it overshadows your good character and influences self-serving choices, your ambition can strangle your integrity edge. The fourth stumbling block is unchecked ambition.

Jack Welch's quote above describes the root of this stumbling block. Before you were a leader, your actions could focus more on yourself. Not to the point of taking advantage of or using others, but you could make choices that solely optimized your personal outcome. However, when you take on the mantle of a leader, it comes with responsibilities. These new responsibilities include supporting, guiding, and looking out for those in your charge. The game changes as soon as you agree to take on leadership responsibilities. You cannot—must not—be solely focused on yourself. You must shift your priorities to focus on the fears, hopes, and dreams of your team members.

Implicit in that responsibility is the requirement that you do not allow your desire for personal gain to influence your actions too much. Prioritizing personal gain over the needs of your team is an illustration of the ambition stumbling block. I have used the example before, likely because it is awful and all too common, but I will use it again. How many of us have heard of a company that is preparing to report record earnings but still executes a reduction in force before the end of the fiscal year? That happens. It is awful, but it happens. Too often, the timing of the unexpected layoff is to achieve compensation-escalating triggers. In these cases, it is often shared as "optimizing business operations," or thinly veiled as "prioritizing strategic investment." Making a decision that impacts your team so negatively, unless absolutely mandatory for the company's survival, could prove that your desire for personal gain has an oversized influence on your decision-making. This is the ambition stumbling block.

Sometimes this stumbling block presents in less dramatic but equally destructive ways, such as thinking, "I know I made a mistake, but the boss thinks Sally did it. All I have to do is keep my mouth shut, and Sally will suffer instead of me." Or, "I know I am not allowed to accept extravagant gifts from vendors, but I have always wanted one of these, and how would anyone find out?"

A friend told me of a time early in his career when everything was going great for him. He was in a job he loved, managing good people, and doing very well. The company held a very high opinion of him. He got a promotion well ahead of the typical schedule. He was motivated by his success and wanted to do everything he could to continue impressing his managers. My friend, Tim, is a conscientious man known for his upstanding character and integrity. He built his career on trust and service to his team members. But early in his career, when his successes started piling up and he wanted to continue to impress, he let his ambition cloud his judgment. Tim told me he started requiring his team members to work late during the week and on weekends so they could reach stretch milestones and blow their numbers out of the water. The extra work was not a requirement, and none of his managers asked him to force the extra time. Tim told me he pressed his team to work outrageous hours because he wanted to continue impressing the company leadership team. Tim said he knew he would look good if his team outperformed expectations.

In the end, a few of the more senior members of Tim's team confronted him about the pace he was setting. They told him about the toll it was taking on the employees and their families, and asked Tim if they could cut back the overtime. They essentially pleaded with him to help them achieve a healthier balance with the amount of overtime they were required to work. Tim finally saw the repercussions of his ambition and made the changes needed to return to a more sensible work schedule. Tim saw the impact of his ambition, but many leaders do not.

The ambition stumbling block can manifest when we allow ourselves to cut ethical corners to ensure a preferred outcome. When ambition and personal gain become the primary motivators, leaders may be tempted to bend or break the rules, compromise their principles, or even engage in unethical behavior. While not as immediately impactful to your team members, taking this path is a steep, slippery slope. Once you "successfully" benefit from ethical compromise, it becomes far more difficult to stop yourself from future compromise.

Unchecked ambition can foster a sense of entitlement and arrogance, and can cause leaders to be less receptive to feedback and criticism. When we are resistant to feedback, we tend to make impulsive decisions. "I am so close to setting the corporate record for quarterly sales, and my boss wants me to take time to explore other options. There's no time. Even if this decision turns out to be bad, that is a problem for next quarter…after I set the corporate record." Getting so focused on achieving your personal goals that you will not listen to good counsel is the ambition stumbling block.

More than anything else, a thorough, unshakable understanding of what is important to you will help keep your ambition in check. This is foundational. It is actually foundational to everything we are talking about in this book. Every stumbling block described in this book will be less of a challenge if you are armed with an absolute, concrete, steel-trap commitment to a clear set of personal values and priorities. When everything is chaos and confusion, when everyone in the world seems against you and allies are nowhere to be found, what do you solemnly believe? When everything is going perfectly, the world is your oyster, and your path seems crystal clear, what does your heart say is your priority?

The ambition stumbling block manifests in many ways. All of the presentations share one characteristic—the leaders are focused solely on immediate rewards while overlooking long-term consequences. When we dismiss the possibility of unexplored, long-term consequences of our actions, we should be suspicious. Unchecked ambition is a terribly sneaky adversary. It sneaks up on us because we have been encouraged to aim high, set lofty personal goals, and pursue them with everything we have. This is good advice until pursuing our goals comes at the expense of the people we have been charged to lead.

AN EXTREME EXAMPLE
OF UNCHECKED AMBITION

Enron was a Houston-based energy company in the late 1990s. They were a major player in the global energy market and, at the start of their downfall, they were the 7th largest corporation in the United States. *Forbes* named them the "Most Innovative Company in America" six years in a row. Enron was a widely respected company with a bright future. All of that changed in 2001.

Early in 2001, the company started reporting losses in many business units and was scrutinized for questionable accounting practices. By the end of 2001, the company filed for bankruptcy and was the subject of many independent investigations. The investigation revealed that Enron executives were manipulating financial records, pressuring employees to perform fraudulent actions, creating fake partnerships, and falsifying corporate results. The consequences of Enron's unethical behavior were far-reaching. Thousands of employees lost their jobs, investors suffered significant financial losses, and the company's reputation was destroyed. Several key executives were convicted of fraud and sentenced to prison.

The senior leaders' motivations for pressuring Enron employees to engage in illegal and unethical practices were driven by personal greed and ambition. Their overwhelming desire to maintain the illusion of success and the positions of power and influence they had achieved led them to decide that breaking a few laws was acceptable. While an extreme example of the steep, slippery slope of ambition, Enron's collapse is a stark reminder of the dangers of unchecked ambition and the erosion of ethical leadership.

PERSONAL IMPACT
OF UNCHECKED AMBITION

When career ambition is left unrestrained and allowed to be the single driving force in a person's life, the impact is felt long before the Department of Justice gets involved in the fraud investigation. The first ones to feel the destructive impact of unhealthy, overwhelming ambition are often the people who are closest to you.

I have a friend, Anthony, whose parents are highly successful and wealthy. His parents excelled in their careers and retired at the top of their fields in the last decade or so. Anthony is in his late forties, married with two wonderful children, and is successful in his own right. Anthony and I discussed what it was like growing up as the only child of such driven parents.

> Growing up, I felt lonely. It was like I was raising myself while my parents were off chasing their careers. I barely saw them. They were always too busy—early-morning meetings, late-night conference calls, business trips that stretched for weeks. It was always something. It was rare to have them around for more than a few minutes a day, and even then, their attention was elsewhere. I have precious few memories of the three of us being together without one of them being constantly interrupted by phone calls and text messages. Even when I was growing up, before cell phones and the internet, they found a way to interrupt our family time. Imagine that: even before it was easy to be distracted by work twenty-four hours a day, my parents found a way to always be focused on work.
>
> When it came to school or activities, they were utterly uninvolved. If I needed help with homework, I was on my own. Parent-teacher conferences? When I was very young,

they'd send my nanny. As I got older, they just skipped them altogether. Baseball, basketball, school plays, even birthdays—they always "meant" to come, but rarely did. By the time I got to middle school, I stopped asking them to come to my games and things because I got tired of hearing excuses. They were always apologetic, insisting they worked all the time "for all of us." It never felt like it was for us; it felt like it was for them and their egos.

Now, our relationship is...strained, to say the least. I don't reach out much, and when I do see them, it's awkward, like we're strangers pretending to be a family. They've tried to reconnect as they've gotten older, but I don't think they understand the damage they did—or maybe they just don't want to acknowledge it. They'll say things like, "You turned out fine, didn't you?" as if that erases the years I spent feeling abandoned and unimportant.

Honestly, I don't know if I'll ever fully forgive them. I know I should, but it's hard to let go of the bitterness when I think about all the stuff they missed. All the stuff I missed. All the times I needed parents and instead got excuses or nothing but silence. I look at them fawning over my kids and cannot help thinking they are hypocrites. They just can't get enough of my kids, but I remember how they were as parents. Family is so important now, but what about when I was growing up? It's still hard.

Sadly, Anthony's story is so common that it is almost a cliche. And yet, this cycle is perpetuated every day by people who have allowed the ambition stumbling block to overwhelm their other priorities. They get so focused on looking good at work and getting that next promotion or next big win that they miss seeing the price they are paying for their success. Often, they don't acknowledge the cost until their careers have ended. Only then do they look around and see what they have become—what their lives and families have become.

In this section, we will discuss some behaviors you can adopt to ensure your ambition remains a positive force in your career journey. We will review a few key activities that will help you maintain the proper focus and help prevent you from rationalizing the unethical pursuit of your personal goals. These recommendations are not magic buttons. They are behaviors that, if you cultivate them and make them part of your life, will help you keep your focus on the things that matter most. When these behaviors become who you are, they will help you keep your ambition as a beneficial force rather than a destructive motivator.

CHANGE YOUR FOCUS

Your personal career ambition can become a stumbling block when you focus on climbing the career ladder to the exclusion of other concerns. When you are overly focused on yourself and your professional success, ambition is one of your primary drivers. When your priorities become one-dimensional, everything you think and do tends to align with that priority.

HEALTHY AMBITION	UNHEALTHY AMBITION
Support team's success	Be the boss
Help others reach their potential	Finish first, always
Be known for integrity	Be the smartest in the room
Cultivate trust and respect	Never fail or look weak
Leave a positive legacy	Protect my image
Improve every day	Win every argument
Serve others	Become famous

Test me on that claim. Do you remember your first "love"? How old were you? Were you in middle school or maybe high school? When that relationship was new, could you think of anything else? What wouldn't you do to be with that person? Did your grades suffer? Did your other friends see less of you? If you were like me, you were wholly focused on your new love to the exclusion of everything and everyone else. Your new relationship was your number one priority to a level that excluded all other concerns. That is the same sort of myopic focus that can turn ambition into a destructive stumbling block.

One method to keep ambition as a positive catalyst, but avoid the stumbling block it can represent, is to change your focus. Purposefully and consciously move your focus to other people and their hopes, dreams, and fears. Move some of your focus to how you might help other people. If we are focused on other people and what we can do to help them, less of our attention is available to fixate on our ambition. Broadly, we can refer to this method as "serving other people."

We discussed the value of serving your team during our discussion on the stumbling block of pride. Serving your team is as easy as focusing on your team members, listening to what they tell you, asking what you can do to help, and then acting on what you hear. Service-minded leaders spend a great deal of time focused on the needs of their team members. These leaders are looking for how they can help their team be more effective and more engaged. Service-minded leaders confront the obstacles and friction their team members encounter and strive to remove the sources. Focus, listen, and act.

A few years ago, Mohammad F. Anwar, Frank Danna, Jeffrey Ma, and Christopher Pitre wrote *Love as a Business Strategy*. Their book provides a powerful, real-life example of how unfettered ambition can be destructive and how focusing on others can be an effective business strategy. I got the opportunity to chat with two of the authors just after I finished reading their book. I shared with them how much their message resonated with me, and I believe it speaks of an epidemic in corporate leadership. Specifically, that selfish executive ambition often destroys company culture and employee engagement. Ultimately, the pandemic of selfish executive ambition erases the integrity edge.

Mohammad Anwar is the CEO of Softway, a technology services company based in Houston, Texas. Softway delivers software development, marketing, and business strategy services. Mohammad began his career as a highly ambitious leader focused solely on growth, profits, and personal success. He writes, "I was obsessed with the idea of success. To me, success meant hitting numbers, winning deals, and showing results. I thought being a good leader meant demanding excellence and pushing people harder." [xi] His drive to climb the ladder and achieve professional success caused him to adopt a controlling leadership style, which led to a toxic work culture at Softway. Mohammad's career journey was hampered by the ambition stumbling block.

Mohammad's excessive focus on personal ambition provided the motivation he needed to found a successful technology company, but ultimately, it was also responsible for nearly destroying it. In time, it became clear that his approach was hurting his company and his relationships with others. Mohammad writes, "I thought I was doing everything right. I was ambitious, driven, and focused. But beneath the surface, my team was unhappy, and the culture was crumbling." [xii] The Softway work environment was marked by fear, distrust, and disengagement among employees. Employees were demoralized, and the company's performance began to decline. He realized that his self-centered priorities were the root cause of these problems. He realized "Unchecked ambition and a lack of accountability create fear-based workplaces where people are afraid to fail, speak up, or innovate." [xiii] Where people are afraid to speak up and take chances, results suffer.

Mohammad made a conscious decision to change his leadership style by prioritizing his employees' well-being, engagement, and growth. He practiced personal vulnerability by admitting his mistakes to his team and sought to rebuild trust. He shifted his attention from personal ambition to understanding and supporting his employees' needs. His journey eventually led him and his leadership team to implement "love" as a business strategy, focusing on empathy, compassion, and inclusivity to create a positive workplace.

As a result of this shift, Softway's culture improved dramatically. Employees felt more engaged, trusted, and valued, which led to higher morale and better performance. Mohammad writes, "When we focus on the well-being of those we lead, we create a culture of belonging, trust, and shared success. Love doesn't mean we abandon results— it means we achieve them the right way." [xiv] Ironically, by focusing on serving others instead of personal ambition, Mohammad not only turned the company around but also achieved the kind of success that his earlier methods couldn't deliver.

Mohammad's story illustrates how focusing solely on personal ambition can have negative consequences, including a toxic work environment, personal dissatisfaction, mistrust, and mental anguish. By consciously redirecting his focus toward serving others, Mohammad transformed his leadership style and his company's culture, ultimately achieving more sustainable and fulfilling success. That is the integrity edge.

Acknowledging, caring about, and working on other people's fears, hopes, dreams, and needs is a vital—perhaps the most vital—aspect of leading with integrity. As Mohammad learned, when you lose your team's trust and engagement, your business aspirations are already lost—it may just take some time for you to see it.

A DIFFERENT KIND OF AMBITION

The ambition stumbling block is different than the other stumbling blocks. The other stumbling blocks—lack of trust, pride, fear, disconnect, toxic culture—can be effectively dealt with, but I am not sure they can be completely and forever removed from your leadership journey. Each of the stumbling blocks can be avoided, and, for a time, they can seem absent from your journey; but when the conditions, people, or pressure changes, the stumbling blocks have a way of showing their ugly faces again. However, the ambition stumbling block alone can be dealt with so completely as to eliminate it as a future source of resistance to your ethical journey.

It's not a trick or a hack that makes this happen. It happens when you fundamentally change the object of your primary ambition. In the example above, Mohammad was initially motivated by "traditional" success markers—title, money, houses, cars, and power. However, when he gained an understanding of what truly mattered to him—serving and caring for others—the siren song of the sports car and bigger house lost its allure.

Mohammad told me, "When I started focusing on others, it impacted my understanding of success—of what success is. It impacted my understanding of everything. My ambition shifted completely. Now success is tied to love and serving humanity."

When Mohammad realized that his foundational, most urgent priority was serving people, the traditional success markers that create the ambition stumbling block became impotent to him. He is no longer motivated by the fancy car, bigger house, or larger paycheck as he once was. Now, he is motivated to positively impact more lives. That ambition is congruent with ethical advancement and leads directly to the integrity edge. When your priorities are in place, ambition will stop being a stumbling block and will become a springboard.

PRIORITIES EXERCISE

I have prepared a multi-step exercise to help you establish a firm foundation on which you can make ethical decisions as your career advances. This exercise should be seen as a permanent tool in your leadership toolbox, specifically designed to be used on yourself. The exercise may seem elementary, but I assure you it will deliver deep and lasting insight into what makes you tick, and why. This exercise will take a fair amount of time (now and in the future) and should not be neglected as you grow. Consider this the price of admission into the ethical career journey you have chosen.

You need to create a list of your priorities. You'll want to think about, meditate, or pray about this topic until you reach a point of certainty—what things, activities, and goals are most important to you?

This isn't a "think about a list in your head" type of thing. Type or write out a list of the people, things, activities, values, and goals that are important to you. This list will change over time, and you almost certainly won't produce a complete list the first time. But you must spend significant time considering what is important to you.

Ideally, you will do this when things are relatively calm and "normal" in your life. If you are dealing with a specific or extreme stressor when you first assemble this list, the list's contents may be overly influenced by the stressor. That's not ideal, but it is better to start this exercise immediately than to wait for your life to calm down. Who knows, perhaps the insights gleaned from this exercise will even help you calm the storm you are currently enduring.

Let's start with people or groups of people:

- What people are important in your life?
- Which people are a priority to you?
- Which groups of people do you spend significant time with in different ways (in-person or apart, live or offline communication)?

Your list should consider family members—partners, parents, siblings, children, grandchildren, and further extended family. Your list should consider important non-family groups as well—coworkers, church family, and friends. Consider adding other important people and groups—political groups, mentors, or mentees.

You should add individuals and groups as you consider them in your mind and actions. If you are equally close to all of your siblings, perhaps "siblings" is an appropriate group. However, if you do not see or talk to your siblings, except your older sister with whom you have a close relationship, perhaps you have two separate entries to your list—"siblings" and "Bethany."

Here is an example of my personal people priorities (not exhaustive):

- Wife
- Children
- Grandchildren
- Friends
- Gary and Alice Smith
- Work—direct reports
- Work—extended team
- Siblings

Now that you have a representative list of the important people and groups in your life, let's focus on hobbies and pastimes:

- What hobbies are important to you?
- If you had a random, surprise three-day weekend, what pastime would you hope to focus on during that weekend?
- What non-work, non-responsibility-related activities do you spend time and money on?

This list of hobbies can include solo endeavors and group pastimes. Perhaps you enjoy walking with your partner but have no interest in walking alone. All good— be specific. Maybe eating, in general, is not a passion, but pizza and wine have a special place in your life—so put them on the list. Things that capture your interest and help you unwind or maximize your "downtime" should be included on this list—running, needlework, model trains, scrapbooking, and collecting Elvis Presley memorabilia are all priority pastimes for someone.

Here is a sample list of my hobby and pastime priorities (not exhaustive):

- Football
- Washington Commanders
- Red wine
- BBQ
- Relaxation
- Baseball
- Watching movies
- Fantasy fiction
- Quiet time
- Reading
- Giving

I would like you to take a little intermission after these first two groups of priorities. I trust you are actually writing these things down or creating a digital list in your preferred application. Simply thinking about these things is insufficient in this exercise. As I mentioned, we are going to work with these lists for a while. We will get deep and detailed. The things we are brainstorming need to be documented for this process to bear fruit.

With people and hobbies knocked out, let's focus on goals and aspirations:

- Are there short or long-term goals that have your attention?
- Is there a place you want to visit or an accomplishment you want to achieve?
- Do you have a vision for where your career is heading?
- Do you have a specific destination in mind for your career?

- When you put your head on the pillow at night, do you think about your progress toward a specific goal that day?
- Is there a goal that you slot into your calendar months in advance to ensure you don't let it sit idle?

This list can go in all sorts of directions. It will end up being a highly personalized list. For instance, the world is full of runners, but they do not all share the same goals. One is hoping to run their first mile. Another is training for their first 5k. For another, it is their first marathon. I was once climbing West Maroon Pass between Crested Butte and Aspen, having gained two thousand feet since 6 a.m., nearing the 12,500 feet pass, when my wife and I were passed by a sixty-something-year-old lady who told us she was hoping to hit her personal record for completing the twenty-six-mile, Four Pass Loop run that day. She told us this as we were trying to suck air into our lungs, doubled over with our hands on our knees, and she passed us, high-stepping at a jog. Goals and aspirations are highly personal—what is meaningful to me (completing the eleven-mile Crested Butte to Aspen West Maroon Pass hike in one day without dying) was scarcely more than a warm-up for that overachieving, high-stepping show-off (I tease, I hope she hit her personal record that day). But her goal would be comical on my list, and my goal wouldn't be worth mentioning on hers.

Your list should include work goals and aspirations—become a manager, get a C-suite role, get a specific certification, or complete a college degree. The goals can be short- and long-term— become a manager (short term) and get a C-suite role (long term).

Your list should include non-work goals and aspirations, like the lady's personal record for the Four Loop Pass. Incidentally, she was not the only person we met that day running the twenty-six-mile loop—just the first. There were three or four others before we made it to Aspen. Shocking, right? Non-work goals can represent endless possibilities—buying a specific sports car, writing a book, and reaching a certain balance in your retirement account are all valid non-work goals.

Here is an example of my prioritized goals and aspirations (not exhaustive):

- Write a book
- Hike every state
- Spend a month in Europe with my wife
- Learn to speak and read Spanish

The final primary category we will focus on is traits and characteristics:

- What personal and behavioral characteristics are important to you?
- What personality traits do you prioritize for yourself and the people you interact with?
- Are there specific behaviors you look for from the people you associate with?
- Is there a way of thinking or acting that significantly shapes your personality or how you engage with the world?

Wow...this one is a little bit tougher. This list is a bit more difficult to draw a box around. I want you to consider the traits that you value most. Is it honesty? Do you value candor? Is it diplomacy? Is it being sociable, or perhaps it is being more reserved? Think about the people you hold in high esteem—do they share a characteristic? Think about when you are most proud of your children—what makes you proud? Think of the way you hope you will be remembered when you leave a room. Which of your traits do you hope resonates the most with the people around you? Do you find a specific behavior highly correlated with long, fruitful friendships?

Here is an example of my trait and characteristic priorities (not exhaustive):

- Faith
- Honesty
- Courage
- Trust
- Peaceful
- Integrity
- Present and engaged
- Growth mindset
- Optimistic

With that section drafted, your initial list is complete. You have brainstormed the people, hobbies, goals, and traits that are important to you. I am fairly certain your list is incomplete, but it is a list. Like they say, "The journey of a thousand miles starts with a single step," or a single list in this case. Schedule time on your calendar to ensure you are able to consider this topic more deeply. Start with an hour of brainstorming. Use what you already created as a seed and add to it. Try not to edit the list as you are creating it. There will be time for that later. In your first session, just explore all the items that come to mind. Go deep.

The result of this exercise should be the most comprehensive list of personal priorities you have ever assembled. The final list will be everything that makes you tick—people, things, behaviors, goals, and dreams. Congratulations, this step, a.k.a. the easiest part, is complete.

Why Are They Important?

After your first or second brainstorming session, you have a healthy list. There may be fifteen, twenty, or fifty words on your list. There is a mix of people, things, activities, feelings, goals, and values. During your brainstorming, you thought a fair amount about these words. You must have, because otherwise the list would be much shorter and not contain the variety it does.

What came to mind when you wrote these things?

When brainstorming, did you consider what each word means to you and why they deserve to be on your list?

The next step in this exercise is to provide details for each word on your list. This is going to take some time. I urge you to give it that time. The value of this exercise does not come from completing the exercise. The value comes from working through the process.

This exercise can become an ongoing part of your personal time. I hope you have time in your schedule to think, plan, and prepare. A time when you work on yourself. The "Why are they important?" step can be an important addition to your prep time.

Schedule some time, thirty to sixty minutes per priority category, over the next several weeks. During this scheduled time, I want you to document why each word is on your list.

- What does that word mean to you?
- Why is it on the list?
- Why is it important?

Continuing from my previous example, these are the details I might provide for a few words I uncovered in my brainstorming:

Wife—I love my wife deeply and completely. She is the most generous and caring person I know. She is the most important person in my life. She is the mother of my children. She is my closest friend. When I imagine the rest of my life, all the best parts involve her. I love laughing with her. I love traveling with her. I love sitting in the house and doing nothing with her. She knows the best and worst things about me. She loves me completely. There is no Rusty without Paulette. She makes me a better man.

Giving—My family and I are blessed. We are healthy—physically and financially. I am compelled to give where I have abundance. Giving time, money, and attention to others is a simple and powerful service that I can provide. When I give to others, I help them in ways they likely cannot help themselves. I help lift them in hopes that they will help lift others. Giving the right thing at the right time to the right person can transform a life.

Football—I have been a football fan since I was a young boy. At this point in my life, football and the Washington Commanders are part of my identity. My friends and family know that I love the game and the team, and it often becomes a topic of conversation. When I was younger, I played—though not well or for long—but I still remember it fondly. There is something about the game that pulls me in. My pulse races when my team or my players do well. On Sunday afternoons and Monday nights, I can't help but wonder how all of the games are going. I love to watch the highlights. I imagine I would have been a good coach or general manager—though I suspect that is just my imagination.

You are not trying to write the perfect description when elaborating on your words. Your goal is to list details about that word that are meaningful to you. Notice in my examples that the details are more a stream of consciousness than a cohesive definition of the word. During this part of the exercise, we want to add context and depth to each word to illustrate what it means to us and why.

When you get to the word or words you placed on the list regarding your professional growth and success, give it the same time and attention as your other words. Take time to dig into why career success is important to you. Is it the money? Is it prestige or power? Detail all the reasons you can think of that make career growth important to you.

How did you feel as you were detailing these words? Often, this exercise will cause people to realize or remember aspects of the important things they have forgotten or have not consciously realized. The process of thinking and writing details about our priorities can help crystalize what is important to us.

When we take time to dig deeper than the surface level, we often discover hidden details. That's the point of this step—take the time to consider why the things we claim are important hold value to us.

What Is Most Important?

At this point, you have developed a list of important things—a relatively easy exercise. You have provided details and context for why each thing is important—a tougher exercise that took time and a fair amount of introspection. The final step in this process is to rank your list.

- What is the most important thing?
- What is the next most important thing?

You can only have one number one and one number two. Do not cheat in this process and choose 1a and 1b.

This step will force you to understand what is most important to you. This step takes time, will likely frustrate you, and requires you to get fully honest with yourself.

When considering your ranking, feel free to group family members as one. This exercise is not about picking your favorite child or parent. From what I can see, there is no upside to that task. For this exercise, it is sufficient to acknowledge where family, in general, falls on your list of priorities. Grouping your family members when considering how you prioritize "family" is perfectly acceptable.

Here are some techniques you can use to rank your priorities:

1. How would my life be impacted if this item or person were not present?
    Example: I would miss BBQ if it were no longer a part of my life. From time to time I would think about brisket and wish I could have it again, but my life would go on.
2. Use paired comparisons. Compare two items at a time. If you had to sacrifice one of the two things, which would you choose?
    Example: Quiet time v. children—I would be willing to sacrifice my quiet time in favor of my children. I deeply value quiet time but will happily interrupt it if my children arrive.
3. How do these things impact your life: your happiness and fulfillment, your personal growth and identity, your relationships and connections, your legacy or long-term aspirations?
    Example: I enjoy baseball, but it plays almost no role in my personal growth, identity, or legacy. On the other hand, my family scores very high in nearly all of these areas of impact.

4. Are there things on your list that are nonnegotiable? *Example:* Faith is a nonnegotiable consideration for many people and should, therefore, be ranked very high.

Determining what is more important between two things you would have said were "most" important can be difficult. In some ways, it may even seem unfair. Is family or integrity more important to you? Perhaps you discover, as you contemplate this list, that you best prioritize your family by determining that you will always act with integrity, which will even color how you engage with your family. In that way you may decide that integrity is a higher priority than family. This does not diminish the value you place on family; it just provides additional context you may have never considered.

What do you decide when you rank "get a C-suite role" with "trust"? Which will you decide is a higher priority, "honesty" or "getting $_____ in my retirement account"?

This exercise will help you build a foundation for making future decisions by directly confronting what is important to you and why. Thinking about your priorities and debating their relative merit with yourself will help you keep your ambition properly framed in the future.

Essentially, this is your time to frame your professional ambition with your other ambitions. Professional ambition can become unchecked when it is considered outside of the context of your other ambitions. If you don't prioritize family, faith, personal values, or hobbies—anything higher than professional success—you are going to find growing your career ethically to be near impossible. These other things—faith, values, and family in particular—are potent catalysts for ethical actions.

Professional ambition can become unchecked when it is considered outside of the context of your other ambitions.

Revisit, Review, and Revise

To maximize this exercise's value, it is important to remind yourself of the answers you prepared. Your work here is only valuable if you can weaponize it against unchecked ambition.

That means having the thoughts you labored over during these exercises available when ambition is threatening your ethical actions. To do this, it's important to keep them top of mind. Spend some of your quiet time thinking about the things that are most important to you. If you journal, get into the habit of writing about these important things from time to time. As I mentioned earlier, make reviewing and reflecting on the truths you documented in this list part of your personal planning and preparation time. The more time you spend with these truths, the more readily they will come to mind when you face the ambition stumbling block.

Finally, revisit this list periodically. Our priorities change over time. New priorities pop up—like grandchildren. Old priorities fall off—like competitive sports. It is expected and proper that your priorities change over time. It is essential to consider the implications of these changes.

Early in my career, I determined that I wanted to be a CIO at a public company before I retired. At the time, I was a first-time manager without a college degree. Setting the audacious goal to become a public company CIO focused my efforts for many years. I was able to complete my degree. I accumulated a bunch of industry certifications.

I pursued advanced degrees and executive certificates. I learned how to lead and manage teams. I pursued promotion after promotion, knowing that I needed to continue growing if I was going to reach my goal. I accomplished my goal in 2021 when Signify Health had its IPO (initial public offering). Since then, I have realized that the CIO title no longer holds the same appeal for me. I am no longer motivated to find the next promotion or the next big thing. My priorities have shifted, and my actions bear it out.

I think the same will be true for you. As you progress in your career, what is most important to you will also change. Keep an eye out for these changes so you can continue to arm yourself with a deep understanding of your priorities. This is the best defense for the ambition stumbling block, and many other stumbling blocks we have reviewed.

SUMMARY

Ambition isn't evil. Ambition is a powerful catalyst and motivator. When personal ambition is properly framed and works in context with all your other priorities, it will make all the difference in your career trajectory. However, when ambition becomes the first or only priority, your dreams of ethical advancement are in jeopardy.

The ambition stumbling block can be avoided. The best defenses against this stumbling block are deep self-reflection and a heart to serve others.

- Change your focus
- Serve your team members
- Beware of small compromises

- Listen to feedback
- Document your priorities
- Revisit and review your documented priorities regularly
- Redefine success in terms that promote ethical decisions

5

THE SILENT KILLER OF GREAT LEADERS
Why Disconnection from Your Team Leads to Disaster

"When leaders stop listening, followers stop talking."

—ANDY STANLEY, *author of* The Next Generation Leader[xv]

I N 2024, Boeing's leadership proudly unveiled plans for future growth and innovation. As part of their strategic plan and a proposed labor agreement, they committed to building their next commercial airplane in the Seattle area—a move they expected would generate excitement and loyalty among their workforce. They included a 25 percent wage increase over four years, certain it would be seen as both generous and forward-looking.

They were wrong. Ninety-four percent of union members voted to reject the offer. Ninety-six percent voted to authorize a strike. That is the definition of disconnected.

The leaders were focused on expansion, innovation, and securing Boeing's future. But their employees were focused on something far more immediate: the realities of stagnant wages, rising living costs, and eroding benefits. While executives were envisioning new aircraft and market dominance, their people were grappling with daily financial pressures and growing frustration.

The disconnect wasn't about vision. It was about awareness. The leadership team misread the room—not because the signals weren't clear, but because they had stopped listening. They underestimated how much the team's present condition mattered.

The Boeing strike of 2024 stands as a powerful reminder: When leaders lose connection with their teams, their leadership effectiveness can be comprised, and their ambitious plans can crumble.

By now, you have likely noticed a pattern. As we walk through the stumbling blocks to ethical advancement, in nearly every case at least one of the recommended protections against the stumbling block pertains to communicating with team members. Many people call the leadership style I focus on "servant leadership." Servant leadership is an excellent moniker for the leadership style and helps explain the repeated references to protecting yourself against the stumbling blocks by communicating with the team.

This leadership style is all about discovering the things holding your team back—their encumbrances—and removing them. This model is built on an understanding that your team members are producing your team's output. As the leader, you are responsible for directing and supporting their efforts. You are responsible for discovering what is slowing them down, causing them to be less effective, or creating friction in the workplace, and removing the causes.

And still, many leaders begin devaluing the connection with their team members as they climb the leadership ladder. As they get to the next rung of the ladder, they decrease the time they spend with their team members. In doing so, they lose touch with their team members and what they are going through. These leaders become so focused on "strategy" and "goals" that their understanding of the people they are guiding lapses.

The disconnect stumbling block is this devaluing of a leader's connection with their team members. Leaders impacted by this stumbling block slowly lose touch with their team members. As the leader disconnects from the team, they lose the insight into the members' experience and, in doing so, lose the ability to serve them effectively. Leadership action that does not focus on service to the team members is a fast track to becoming the self-absorbed, unethical leader that we want to avoid being.

This section will focus on core leadership tools to help you avoid the disconnect stumbling block. I suspect few of these tools will be new to you. The point of this section isn't to share novel approaches to connecting with your team members. Instead, this section provides insights into how you might improve the effectiveness of the tools you already use. We will focus on the three items below:

1. How to effectively communicate with your team members.
2. Different meetings to support different outcomes.
3. Feedback. It is vital but can be challenging to acquire consistently.

There is nothing mysterious about connecting with your team members. It takes time. It takes commitment. It takes patience. The connections do not happen overnight, and each connection is different. What works for connecting with one person may not work for connecting with the next team member. To avoid the disconnect stumbling block, you must embrace finding connection with your team members as your mission—a key component of your winning leadership model. Once you establish those connections, you must continue to press into them. You must continue to cultivate the connections and keep them fresh. Let's sharpen the tools you will use to establish and maintain these valuable connections.

FOSTERING PSYCHOLOGICAL SAFETY

When you communicate with your team members, there is one incontrovertible truth I want you to think about. You cannot interact with an employee who reports to your organization—directly to you or to one of your subordinate leaders—and not be the boss in the conversation. I know, you're thinking, "That's obvious, Rusty." Obviously, if you are the boss, you will be the boss in every conversation. Consider the implications of that fact.

Let's say you have a casual conversation with an individual contributor who reports to a manager who reports to you. You hope to have a friendly, low-key conversation. You anticipate an inconsequential conversation about small things to help establish a connection with the individual. But the employee you are speaking with is talking to "the boss's boss." In most cases, there is nothing "low-key" about the conversation in their mind. While the conversation will likely remain friendly, the employee will often be conflicted by the dichotomy of "talking about small, inconsequential things" and the weight of talking to the boss's boss.

As much as you want the individual contributor to connect with you and feel free to just talk, in many cases, the employee will need some help warming up to that mode of conversation.

However, if we want the team member to engage in a meaningful conversation, there is often a more significant challenge. Imagine a time when, over several conversations with an employee, you have established a connection with a team member. You have graduated from the initial uncomfortable conversation to a few more natural interactions. The employee was initially apprehensive about talking to the boss's boss about small, inconsequential things, but after a few interactions, they warmed up to the idea, and a decent connection was established. Now, we want to press into that connection to hear what the employee is experiencing as they perform their job. Now, we want to leverage the connection we have established to hear what is going well for the employee and what is causing issues.

Asking employees to open up about their work experience with the boss or the boss's boss—especially asking them to talk about their challenges—is a tall ask. As I stated, it is impossible for you not to be the boss or boss's boss, especially when having leadership present for a discussion causes additional angst and apprehension. Employees need to feel safe and valued before making themselves vulnerable. The need to feel safe and valued as employees is often referred to as "psychological safety."

Psychological safety is a term used to describe a situation in which team members believe it is safe to take risks. It describes a team dynamic in which team members are not afraid they will be subjected to negative repercussions for asking questions, making mistakes, delivering bad news, or sharing their opinions. If you want to be a leader who serves your team members and leads with integrity, you must establish psychological safety in your team.

In many ways, this book is about how a leader establishes psychological safety for their teams. If you avoid the stumbling blocks described in this book, you will almost certainly establish a team dynamic that is characterized as "safe." To encourage this psychological safety in one-on-one and small group communication, focus on three personal behaviors: transparency, vulnerability, and active listening.

Transparency

If you distill it down to the most basic level, communicating with transparency means not playing games with your team members when you speak with them. Be honest. If there are issues, concerns, or risks, do not claim there aren't any. Sometimes you will have information that you are not at liberty to share—the team members know that. Telling them "We are working on some things in that space, but I really cannot share any details right now" is far more satisfying than "No. Nothing is going on. Everything is fine." If you cannot share something, tell them you cannot. But, if you are at liberty to share information, share that information.

Transparency is characterized by open and complete sharing, not withholding anything—good or bad—that you are authorized to share. Finally, do not make them guess what you are talking about. Speak plainly. Be clear. Long, flowery monologues can be difficult to follow sometimes. You don't want to lose your listener because you didn't get to the point. Clear and concise beats long and descriptive when it comes to communicating with your team.

Vulnerability

Being vulnerable in your communication means sharing your thoughts, feelings, and experiences honestly, even when they are imperfect or challenging. Your team members know that you are human and that humans make mistakes, have emotions, and face challenges. If you try to hide your experiences, you can come off as untrustworthy or unbelievable.

Sharing personal ordeals and challenges you have faced in your career and personal life can help the team members relate to you. Tell them about the time you messed up and caused the company to miss a deadline. Tell them that you had to take the bar exam twice before you passed it. Share with them your frustrations of getting passed over for a promotion. It will help you get past the "boss" barrier.

Look for opportunities to admit the mistakes you have made to your team members. Sharing your mistakes has many benefits. It shows the team you are willing to take responsibility for your actions, which encourages them to do the same. Admitting mistakes shows you are willing to acknowledge and learn from your errors. It encourages the team members to look at missteps differently. It establishes a mindset that some good can come out of a blunder if we learn a lesson. Mistakes are rarely a good thing, but they can be used as a learning experience. We often learn and grow far more when things don't go as expected than we do when everything goes according to our plans.

Being vulnerable in your communication with your team members means being willing to show your emotions—positive and negative. Team members may find it easier to connect with you if they see you exhibit common human feelings. Leaders who maintain a stoic, emotionless demeanor can be difficult to empathize with. They might find communicating with such leaders intimidating and are less likely to be fully engaged.

Active Listening

The final personal behavior that may help you get past the "boss" communication barrier is active listening. Active listening means being fully engaged with whoever is speaking. It means listening to fully understand the speaker's message. It isn't just hearing the words—it also includes gleaning mood, tone, emotion, and intent from nonverbal cues to get the full message. Practicing active listening is characterized by maintaining eye contact and not becoming distracted by your phone or any of the thousands of notifications we get during an average day.

The "active" part of active listening refers to the things you do when you are engaged in conversation. Use signals—nodding and simple verbal cues like "uh huh" and "yep"—to let the speaker know you are following along and understand what they are saying. Asking clarifying questions to ensure you understand the speaker's message is a wonderful tool in the "active listening" toolbox. Paraphrasing and summarizing what the speaker said in your own words is another critical active listening tool. It ensures you have captured the speaker's intended message.

Practicing these three behaviors—transparency, vulnerability, and active listening—when engaging with your team will help you establish the connection you need to best serve them. Continual service to your team is the best way to ensure you stay on the path of ethical advancement.

DIFFERENT MEETINGS FOR DIFFERENT OUTCOMES

Like it or not, communicating and connecting with your team members means having meetings. Meetings get a bad rap for being wasteful time sinks. Well, to be clear, they get this reputation because they are too often completely wasteful. The problem with meetings being time sinks is so pervasive that many more qualified authors have written millions of words on how to run useful meetings. This section is not a primer on how to run effective meetings. I recommend you find a few meeting-effectiveness improvement texts and take their lessons to heart.

Because, like it or not, you will need to have some meetings. Lots and lots of meetings. Large meetings, small meetings, and one-on-one meetings. Relationships are built during human interactions. In business, many—perhaps most—of the human interactions we experience are during one meeting or another.

In the context of avoiding the disconnect stumbling block, I will focus on three specific types of meetings: team meetings, one-on-one meetings, and personal check-in meetings. Each of these three meeting types represents a prime opportunity to enhance your connection with your team and help avoid the disconnect stumbling block.

Team Meetings

Team meetings are invaluable platforms for leaders to maintain a strong connection with their team members. These gatherings help create a sense of unity and alignment, ensuring everyone is on the same page regarding the team's vision and mission. You can inspire your teams to work toward a shared purpose by openly communicating goals and expectations. Moreover, team meetings create a space for open dialogue and collaboration among team members. When you actively listen to your team members' perspectives, you can demonstrate genuine interest and support, fostering a positive and productive work environment. This helps the team members see you as someone interested in helping them be more productive rather than just the "boss."

One-on-One Meetings

One-on-one meetings with your team members can be a game-changer in avoiding the disconnect stumbling block. They are especially effective if you extend the one-on-one meetings beyond your direct reports. I know, I know. You're thinking, "Do you have any idea how many people I have

on my team? There is no way I could have regularly scheduled one-on-ones with all of them." I disagree.

You can extend your one-on-ones to every level of your
organization; you just have to be organized and diligent
with your efforts. You will not have one-on-ones with every team member every week. But what if you had one-
on-ones with your direct reports each week and with your
extended team less frequently? The exact frequency that is
possible depends on the size of your team, but could you
commit to speaking with each team member once a quarter? Is that possible? It will take planning and some sacrifice, but the dividends of knowing your team members
and staying connected to them could be immeasurable.

One-on-one meetings are not the same as most of your
other meetings. These meetings are not focused on your
initiatives, projects, or deadlines. These meetings are focused on the person you are meeting with. The meeting is
about their performance, career, fears, hopes, and dreams.
The one-on-one is about whatever they need you to pay
attention to—it is not about you or your priorities. If you
want to talk about a project deadline, schedule a different
meeting. This meeting is about your team member.

Some of the standard meeting conduct rules are dou-
bly important in one-on-ones. These meetings will be
less than useful if the person you are meeting with gets
the impression you would rather be somewhere else. For
one-on-ones to succeed, the person you are meeting with
needs your undivided attention, and they need to see that
you are genuinely interested in the discussion.

Schedule the meeting and protect it on your calendar.
Do everything you can to keep from moving or resched-
uling the one-on-one. When you reschedule a meeting,
you can give the impression that something more important came up. While that might be true occasionally, you

should protect one-on-ones as a critical meeting that takes priority over other meeting types. Protecting a scheduled one-on-one meeting time will not always be possible, but you should do everything possible to avoid sacrificing a one-on-one.

When you are in the one-on-one, focus on the person you are meeting with. Make eye contact. Practice active listening—give nonverbal cues that you are following along, ask follow-up questions, and restate what you hear. Allow yourself to be transparent and vulnerable when you find an opportunity. The person you are meeting with is more likely to be honest and vulnerable with you if they see you are willing to do the same. And finally, most importantly, when you are in a one-on-one, PUT YOUR DEVICES AWAY. Nothing says "I would rather be doing something else" more clearly than scrolling through your phone or checking a text message when the other person is talking. Don't do that. It is rude, and it will sink any chance you have for a useful one-on-one.

Personal Check-Ins

Personal check-in meetings are a hack for avoiding disconnection. If you can get this right, it will completely change how well you connect with your team members. Best of all, this method works great regardless of your team size. Here is how this meeting mode works:

- Make a list of every employee in your extended team (not just direct reports). Make sure the list includes their job function.
- Use Slack, Microsoft Teams, or whatever tool you have for direct messaging to reach out to one of them. Just send something sincere, like, "Good

morning, <employee's name>! I hope you are doing well. I have been struggling to find ways to have meaningful conversations with everyone in our organization. I thought I would give this one-on-one Slack conversation a try. How are you doing? What's on your mind? How can I help?"

- Once the team member responds—and they will respond—use that as the first words of a real conversation. Let the team member guide the discussion. Be personable. Be honest. Be sincere. This does not need to be a prolonged conversation for it to be meaningful. It just has to be sincere.
- Rinse and repeat this process until you have completed a personal check-in meeting with every team member.
- When you get to the last name on the list, update your list to capture anyone who has joined or left your team since you created the last list, and start over.

This method works if you work it. You don't have to commit to talking to all 100 team members—or 1,000 team members—this month. Just commit to reaching out to each person on your team. And then keep your commitment. It might take months or even multiple quarters for you to contact each team member. That's okay. Without this connection hack, you would never have reached out to every team member.

Personal check-in conversations create a touch point with people you have never engaged with in person. Proactively reaching out to the team member and letting them know you know them and see them helps the employee believe you care about them. Some employees will even use this initial outreach as an invitation for them to reach out to you in the future. That is a win. Take advantage of these engagements to avoid the disconnect stumbling block.

HOW TO GET HONEST FEEDBACK

Soliciting feedback from your team members is one of the most important things you can do to ensure you serve your team effectively. Without such feedback, a leader is left to guess what their team members want and need from them. It can be difficult to get candid feedback from your team members. If you are the senior leader, you cannot be in a room with your team without being their boss. There is no way to enter a conversation or hold a meeting without bringing your corporate power with you. You can try, but the team knows, and often cannot forget long enough to provide the feedback you desperately need.

While it is challenging to get candid suggestions from your team members, it is not impossible. There are things you can do to improve your chances of getting feedback from your team members. In the following sections, I will discuss beneficial behaviors and tools that can help you collect valuable feedback. I will even share a couple of feedback hacks that might be the final nudge your team members need to share their opinions.

One important note before we get into the feedback collection tools—none of these recommendations will move the needle with your team members unless you have already started laying the foundation we have been discussing throughout this book. At the core of any team's reluctance to share valuable feedback is an unspoken concern—perhaps even a fear—that sharing what they think will negatively impact their employment: "If I say what I really think, things could get very bad for me here." If you are going to have any success soliciting input from your team members, you must start by cultivating a trusting and trustworthy working environment. You must prove to your team that you can be trusted and value each of your team members. Without this foundation, there is practically no chance you will successfully collect feedback from your team members.

Assuming you have worked to establish a team culture of trust and respect, let's move on to the feedback behaviors and tools.

Patience

I think I might be starting with the most difficult of the beneficial behaviors. If you are going to find success in your attempts to solicit feedback from your team members, you are going to have to practice patience. Your team is probably not going to open up with the juiciest nuggets of feedback when you first ask. Your team might respond to your heartfelt request for feedback with deafening silence. Stay the course; do not be deterred.

You don't know what their previous leaders were like. You may not know how their previous leaders treated them and what impact that treatment has on your team's ability to trust leadership. Your team might have a difficult time trusting you and believing you want to talk with them to improve outcomes. Too many of your team members may have witnessed former leaders weaponize feedback they received, turning it against the very people who were courageous enough to deliver it. You can bet some of your team members have dealt with things like this. But remember, your team's feedback is valuable enough for you to endure the uncomfortable, often frustrating, process of collecting it.

Many years ago, I was Director of Infrastructure Operations for a US-based software company. I managed a team of roughly sixty people, including both managers and individual contributors, working in multiple locations across the United States. As my team grew, my personal interaction with the individual contributors waned. I knew this would become a problem if I didn't do something about it. I devised a foolproof plan. Based on the premise that the extended team had things they wanted to share, I blocked off one hour every Tuesday and Thursday morning and afternoon as "office hours." This time was reserved for ad-hoc, one-on-one discussions with anyone on the team on any topic they chose. All they had to do was send a meeting reminder to me, and I would show up and discuss whatever was on their mind. I blocked out four hours weekly to ensure I was available to everyone who wanted to talk.

With my calendar prepared, I introduced the new "office hours" in a monthly meeting that included all the team members. I explained the importance of the meetings, saying, "I want to hear what's on your mind and make sure I am available to talk with each of you. I encourage the team to book time for anything. Even if you just want to talk about football." I invited everyone on my extended team to take advantage of the time as frequently as they wished. Fool. Proof. Plan.

For six months I reminded my managers. During each of the subsequent monthly meetings, I encouraged the extended team: "The office hours are yours. Use them for anything that is on your mind." I ensured the entire team knew this opportunity was available to them.

Six months. That is twenty-six weeks. Four hours per week for twenty-six weeks is 104 hours. Guess how many of those 104 hours were booked with one-on-one discussions after six months? Go ahead. Guess.

Zero. I kept the opportunity highly visible and kept the time protected for six months. During that time, nobody on my extended team took advantage of the office hours. "Office hours" was a complete failure. Ultimately, booking time on your boss's boss's calendar is a bridge too far.

After I scrapped the "office hours" experiment, I discussed the failed program with one of the senior individual contributors. He told me he had things he might have liked to talk about, but he never thought they were important enough to book the time. He said it felt odd to book time with the director over something that is probably only important to him. UGH! That was hard to hear.

Your team has things they want to get off their chest. They have ideas they think might be helpful. Things are happening that they are not happy about and they would like changed. They have opinions they would love to share, but just aren't comfortable speaking up. For some, it is fear. For others, it is a lack of confidence. For others, it is just not seeing the right opportunity to say something.

The thing preventing your team members from offering feedback is different for each person. Your approach to collecting their feedback needs to be flexible. Not every approach will work for every person. As I have demonstrated with my brilliant "office hours" approach, some of your ideas won't work for anyone. Keep trying. Stay patient and keep trying.

Hear Their Thoughts

Your goal in developing this connection with your team members is to hear their thoughts. What are they struggling with? What accomplishments are they excited about? What is creating friction for them as they try to do their job? What resources do they need to do their jobs? If you know these things, you can serve them better. After all, how will you be able to effectively support your team if you don't know what they are struggling with? You would have to guess. Hearing the challenges directly from your team is much more effective than guessing.

However, not everything your team tells you is going to be instructive. Sometimes, your team members will share irrelevant things. Sometimes they will share personal things that are more a function of their style than evidence of a problem to be solved. Occasionally, they will be critical of something you are passionate about. At times, they will be adamant about an idea you know is deeply flawed.

In all of these cases, you need to try to be receptive. Meet their feedback with gratitude. Do not feel you need to react immediately to their thoughts or ideas. In most cases, you should receive the feedback without challenging it. It is appropriate to ask clarifying questions and seek additional details. However, it is almost always a mistake to offer a critique of their input as soon as you hear it. Providing immediate critique on someone's observations gives the impression that you are not listening, that you don't want a different point of view, or, worse yet, that you don't care about them. Moreover, when you criticize an employee's feedback immediately, you harm your chances of receiving continued feedback.

Be receptive. That doesn't mean agreeing with everything the employee shares. Being receptive means that you honestly consider everything they share. When your employee shares feedback that doesn't match your understanding or expectations, believe the employee. Believe that the critique they are sharing is sincere. Again, this doesn't mean you are agreeing with them. It simply means that you acknowledge every coin has two sides; every picture can be viewed from many angles. Believe the employee means what they are saying and consider how or why their point of view disagrees with yours. This is the golden feedback you are looking for most—the feedback that causes you to realize the blind spots in your perspective and experience.

A Consistent Part of Team Culture

The final behavior I want to mention that will help you create meaningful connections with your team members is consistency. If you reach out once a quarter for feedback, don't be surprised if it is difficult. When you present your teams with infrequent feedback opportunities, it often leads to the team being inexperienced with providing comments. Inexperience leads to being uncomfortable and uncertain. Uncertainty and discomfort have prevented a lot of valuable feedback from being delivered over the years. If we want to empower our teams to deliver valuable criticism, we must be consistent with the opportunities.

Instead of only scheduling feedback collection a few times each year, make collecting and discussing feedback a regular part of your team's culture. There are some situations where collecting evaluations is obvious and expected—start there.

During the standardized corporate employee performance review process, feedback collection is standard. Don't just go through the motions—lean into the process. Make it clear that you value the process, spend time making it useful, and encourage feedback about the previous period.

When a project or initiative ends, schedule a "lessons learned" or "retrospective" session. Schedule the session as soon as possible after the project's completion. Look for things that went well—tasks, processes, and tools. Ask about things the team found challenging. Ask the team about what they thought was missing from the project.

Perhaps your team was responsible for responding to a critical incident or business interruption event (like a hurricane, fire, or earthquake)—these are perfect times to get the team together to talk about what went well, what was challenging, and what could be done to help the next event go smoother. Disaster responses like this can be traumatic and frightening events. Schedule the "after action" conversation to occur as soon as possible after the disaster response is completed. In most cases, it will help the feedback get started and flow well if you are willing to be the first to talk about how you felt during the event. By going first, you make being frightened acceptable and normal. Others will be more comfortable sharing if you are vulnerable.

Instituting a new process or adopting a new product or service can offer opportunities to solicit "user acceptance" feedback. Get the impacted team together, show them the new thing, and ask for their thoughts. Make it clear that you are asking for their points of view so the process, product, or service can be improved before it is launched. Help the team members understand that their role in this "user acceptance" is to highlight the things that might be a problem when the process, product, or service is launched. Help them understand that, while the development team did their best to develop a valuable new process, product, or service, the team members you gathered are uniquely positioned to help the company—more specifically, to help you—avoid launching a process, product, or service that has a bunch of problems. You are counting on them. Their feedback is the final line of defense between a successful launch or a disastrous one.

Beyond these clear opportunities to solicit feedback, consider using one-on-ones to gather assessments. As previously discussed in this section, one-on-one meetings are a vital part of employee-manager connections. When executed correctly, these meetings can be a foundational building block for growing a proper relationship with your team members. These meetings are also a golden opportunity to normalize employee-to-manager feedback. You may have to ask for feedback on particular topics. You can guide the conversation with opening questions and explanations, but the feedback only happens when you stop talking.

Virtual Daily Stand-up

A feedback tool I have been using for many years is the "virtual daily stand-up." The "daily stand-up" is a standard daily meeting used by practitioners of many agile frameworks. The original daily stand-up is a short meeting (no longer than fifteen minutes), ideally at the start of each day, that asks all participants to share what they worked on yesterday, what they are planning to work on today, and what is preventing them from progressing. It is designed for teams to quickly share what is finished, what is next, and what is blocking them. While this daily stand-up meeting is typically used by agile development teams, I have co-opted the design for my entire technology team.

I use our company instant messaging tool—Slack or Microsoft Teams—to facilitate a daily touchpoint with all of my team members. At the start of each day, every team member is asked to post "Yesterday, Today, and Blockers" in a shared channel. The activity should not take each team member more than a few minutes to complete, and since it is collected in the messaging tool, the meeting is asynchronous—each member completes the activity when it is convenient for them. The result is a summarized list of the things the team worked on yesterday, the things they hope to work on today, and my coveted list of feedback on what is not going well.

The "Blockers" list is the pot of gold at the end of the virtual daily stand-up rainbow. Pay close attention to the blockers list and lend your power, influence, experience, and authority to removing the blockers your team lists, and watch the feedback flow. The virtual daily stand-up, in particular the stated blockers, is a low-effort method for weaving the feedback thread throughout your team's culture. Before you know it, the idea of identifying blockers loses its mystique, and you are presented with a golden opportunity to connect with your team members by helping them remove their roadblocks.

Anonymous and Attributed Surveys

Surveys, both anonymous and attributed, can be powerful tools for leaders to gather valuable feedback from their employees. Surveys provide a structured way to solicit input from your teams. When used well, they can enhance communication, build trust, and foster a culture of transparency and accountability.

Surveys can be anonymous or attributed. Attributed survey responses are linked to a named submitter, while anonymous surveys collect feedback without attributing the responses to an individual. Both types of surveys can help collect feedback and establish a more meaningful connection with team members.

Anonymous surveys can encourage employees to provide honest input without fear of reprisal or judgment. This can be particularly valuable for addressing sensitive or controversial issues. Team members may be more likely to share concerns or challenges when they know their identity remains anonymous.

Attributed surveys can foster a sense of accountability and ownership among employees. When their names are attached to their responses, they are more likely to feel invested in the feedback process. Attributed surveys can help build stronger relationships between leaders and team members by facilitating open and direct communication.

Whether you decide to use an anonymous survey or an attributed survey, there are some best practices you should follow to get the most value from your experience.

- Decide what you hope the survey will deliver. Define the specific goals of the survey and communicate them clearly to the team. This will help ensure that the feedback collected is relevant and actionable.
- If using anonymous surveys, clearly communicate the measures taken to protect the confidentiality of the respondents. Consider using a third-party service or facilitator to execute the survey to provide an additional insulation layer between you and the survey taker.
- Ensure that the feedback collected is analyzed and addressed promptly. This will demonstrate a commitment to accountability.
- Close the loop with your team members by sharing what the team shared in the survey. Share the raw data and the analysis you perform. When the team hears the survey results, it can help them see the value of providing feedback.
- Develop an action plan based on the survey analysis. What will you do with the feedback? Decide on some actions and commit to the team to work on these things.

360-Degree Feedback

A comprehensive evaluation process that collects feedback from multiple sources, including peers, subordinates, superiors, and sometimes external stakeholders is called 360-degree feedback. This multi-faceted approach provides a more holistic view of an individual's performance and development needs. This approach to feedback collection can deliver insights that might otherwise be missed when some sources are not questioned.

Be clear with all participants that their opinions will be gathered by an independent third party who has been engaged to allow all feedback to be collected, analyzed, and completely anonymized before it's shared with you. Ensure that all feedback is handled confidentially and that participants' identities remain anonymous.

Including team members in the 360-degree feedback often has a dramatic and lasting impact on the individuals who are included in the request. There is something about the boss organizing an independent third party to ask about the boss's strengths and weaknesses that is empowering, and almost flattering in some cases. Don't underestimate the value of this ongoing, engaging effect when selecting team members to participate in the 360-degree feedback. Resist the urge to include only high performers from your team in the feedback request. Consider adding team members who struggle with engagement or are historically reluctant to offer their thoughts.

Start, Stop, Continue

One method for gathering quality feedback from your team members is the "start, stop, continue" approach. "Start, stop, continue" is a simple but powerful method for gathering feedback.

In a one-on-one meeting with one of the people in your organization, ask them the following questions:

1. What is one thing I am not doing currently to assist you that you would like me to *start* doing?
2. What is one thing I do that you do not see as helpful, which you would like me to *stop* doing?
3. What is one thing I currently do that you find to be valuable and would like me to *continue* doing?

You should encourage them to be honest. Make sure they know they have permission to identify actions, behaviors, and tendencies that you have shown—or not shown—in the past when they answer the question.

Recently, I introduced this approach to soliciting feedback to a group of managers and directors who directly reported to me. My purpose in sharing the approach was to help my team's leaders lean into soliciting and acting on feedback from their teams. I had not planned on directing the "start, stop, continue" to me, but when I introduced the approach, I discovered that my team had been withholding important feedback from me. I suspect they were not consciously withholding the feedback, but they felt like they did not have the appropriate venue to share their "please, stop doing that" feedback. It can be challenging to tell the boss they are doing something that makes your job harder.

We were on a video conference call when I introduced the approach. I shared the "start, stop, continue" name and then explained each type of feedback. When I got to "stop," I could see smiles on the faces of a couple of my team's leaders. I immediately realized that the team was thinking of things they wanted me to stop doing. I asked one of my directors what he was smiling about.

"Rusty, you have a couple of habits on video conference meetings that make me and the other leaders nervous. You have a habit of pacing when you put your standing desk in the raised position. Also, you tend to rest your head in your hands sometimes. Both of these cause us to wonder what you are thinking. It seems like you are upset or disappointed—or worse—when you do these things."

How about that feedback? My desire to stand during the day and my mannerisms when thinking and engaging were causing my leadership team anxiety. I failed to consider how these actions might look on video, and without the feedback from my leadership team, I would likely still be doing these things today.

"Start, stop, continue" is a simple approach that almost gamifies feedback for the team members. It spells out a specific request for feedback that otherwise might remain locked behind their apprehension and uncertainty about how you might react. Now they have an active draw on those things that serve to decrease the apprehension.

The "continue" feedback will feel like recognition of things you are doing well.

The "start" feedback might feel like you have fallen short of delivering full value to the employee or team.

The "stop" feedback will feel like a spotlight has been placed on all the ways you have messed up.

Once they provide feedback for any of these questions, thank them. Make certain they know you appreciate the feedback. Tell them you realize it is sometimes difficult to share constructive criticism with leadership, and doing so takes courage. You want to establish a positive response to this feedback, or you risk never getting this sort of candid input in the future.

Now that you have some feedback, review it with the person who provided it. Ask clarifying questions. Ask for examples and specific times things did—or did not—happen. Make sure to establish a shared understanding as to why a specific action, behavior, or tendency is helpful or harmful.

Once you are sure you understand the feedback given, set an action plan. Let the person who gave the feedback know what you intend to do with their assessment. If you are ready to take action related to the feedback, tell them and make a commitment. If you require more time to consider your response, tell them and commit to a time and date for follow-up. You should leave the "start, stop, continue" discussion with a shared understanding of what you are going to do with the feedback.

If you are leading a group where trust is absent or has yet to be established, I recommend starting with "continue" feedback. Add "start" and "stop" when the participants have established a level of trust.

The Most Important Question

Todd Henry is a bestselling author and international speaker who consults on creativity, productivity, passion for work, and generating brilliant ideas. He talks about the importance of good leadership in cultivating an environment where team members can flourish. He knows your people have an opinion about your leadership and the direction the team is heading—they just don't always feel comfortable telling the boss. He has a simple recommendation for how you can help encourage your team members to tell you what they see.

Mr. Henry suggests the most important question a leader can ask their team members is, "What is something obvious that I am missing?" It is a simple question that packs a punch. This question gets beyond the rhetorical,

"Is there anything else?" that typically results in a simple "no." The question posits that the leader knows there is something they are missing and gives the team members permission to share what they see. In many cases, this permission can be sufficient to help the team members get past their apprehension and share.

"What is something obvious that I am missing?" is a brilliant question. It is a simple offer of vulnerability—"I know there is something I am unaware of." In this way, it cuts through the veil of infallibility that many leaders attempt to cultivate and publicly acknowledges that you are not all-knowing—that you don't have all the answers. It helps the team members see that they might be part of the solution: "I know there is something I am unaware of. Do you see it? Can you tell me what I am missing?"

The Meeting Plant

Consider the following situation: You have a topic you have been thinking about and want your team members to chime in. You need their input. You want your team members to tell you what you are missing. You are sure your team members trust you, but how can you get the candid feedback you desperately need? Try setting up a "meeting plant."

Before you meet with the team, pull one of your trusted team leaders aside. This leader should be senior-level and influential among her peers. Tell her you are going to be presenting a new topic in the meeting and that you need her to disagree with something in your message. Ask her to be your plant. Ask her to find a piece of the presentation to challenge during the meeting. If you let her in on the "meeting plant" idea, it will help her understand why you are asking, and it might help her overcome any reluctance she is experiencing to provide candid feedback.

I have used this method many times. The most incredible thing happens when the first person in the room disagrees or challenges the leader and does not get shut down or reprimanded for the disagreement.

Before the meeting plant challenges one of your ideas, all the heads in the room nod along, seemingly agreeing with your every word. The nods are not actually evidence of agreement. In many cases, the nods are actually visual encouragement for you to move the meeting along because they have no intention of speaking up. However, if you let the first feedback land and receive it well, the floodgates will open. Something happens to the team members' reluctance when they see their peer successfully navigate the feedback request. Seeing the success of their peer unlocks their feedback. It is as if they were looking for evidence that it is safe to disagree, and the meeting plant provided that evidence.

People want to be helpful and share their points of view; they just need to know they are safe to do so. Having a plant in the room is not dishonest; it is a meeting productivity hack. It is a feedback hack.

To set up a successful meeting plant, find an influential member of the discussion group and encourage them to find something to disagree with in an important meeting. Ask your plant to open a debate on something you share in the meeting, but let the "something" be up to your plant. It needs to be authentic.

When your plant disagrees, participate in an honest and open debate. Thank the meeting plant for the feedback. Watch what happens to some of the folks who previously felt unsafe. Hopefully, some will join in the discussion. Perhaps some will even voice their own disagreements or counterpoints once they see it is encouraged. Most importantly, some will remember the debate and the positive way it was received and will have more confidence in future discussions.

Do the following to ensure it is not just meeting theater:

1. Let the "meeting plant" choose what they challenge.
2. Do not rehearse.
3. Discuss the plant's input honestly. Agree where you agree and disagree where you disagree.
4. Don't feel like you have to adopt the idea the plant presents. The discussion should result in a better solution.
5. Encourage other attendees to join the discussion.
6. Don't always use the same plant.

SUMMARY

The disconnect stumbling block is a subtle compromise encourager. Once leaders become disconnected from their team, they become more susceptible to many other stumbling blocks. Without the connection, effectively serving the team becomes almost impossible. Pride can take a foothold without the team's feedback, and fear can run rampant. And forget about trust—when the team realizes you do not value them or their points of view, trust is off the table.

It takes focus and commitment from you, but the disconnect stumbling block can be avoided.

- Remember that, regardless of how hard you try, you will always be the boss when talking with your team members. There is nothing you can say or do that changes that.
- You must help team members feel safe when talking to you. You will still be the boss, but your

communication will be more effective if team members feel safe.

- Don't play games with your team members. Be clear and transparent when you speak with them. Making them guess what you are after will increase their unease and hamper your communication.
- Be vulnerable with your team members. Let them know you have struggles and concerns. Drop the perfection facade and help them see you as a normal person.
- When they finally decide to share with you— LISTEN. Practice active listening. Ensure they know you are engaged, you hear them, understand them, and care about their point of view.
- Use team meetings and one-on-one meetings intentionally. Team meetings are to get everyone on the same page and pulling in the same direction. One-on-ones are to help cultivate more profound personal connections with team members.
- Use personal check-ins to underscore your care and concern for your team members. Find a way to "talk" to every team member.
- Collective feedback is hard. Practice the feedback behaviors—patience, receptiveness, and consistency—to increase your effectiveness.
- Take advantage of the feedback tools—surveys and 360-degree feedback—to unlock reluctant feedback. Use "start, stop, continue," the most important question, and the meeting plant to help your team members get past their reluctance to share their points of view.

6

TOXIC CULTURE V. INTEGRITY EDGE
What to Do When the Culture is Working Against You

"The way to change culture is to change behavior."

—JON KATZENBACH, *organizational culture expert and author of* The Wisdom of Teams[xvi]

HAVE YOU HEARD THE SAYING, "Culture eats strategy for breakfast"? It is a common saying that is often inaccurately attributed to Peter Drucker. The source of this saying remains unknown, but the premise is true. No strategy is profound or brilliant enough to succeed if the culture of a group is unwilling or unable to focus on its execution. Since people are required to execute a strategy, the team's culture will determine how, or even if, the strategy is approached.

Culture is not static. It can change over time. Positive, supportive cultures are negatively impacted when destructive, selfish actions taken by employees and leaders are ignored, tolerated, or rewarded. Toxic cultures can be positively impacted when the actions that have made them toxic—bullying, harassment, fear-based motivation, lack of ownership, or hundreds of other negative behaviors—are no longer tolerated, and those who use these methods are corrected or punished. Over time, if the accepted actions within a company are changed, a corresponding change in the company's culture will follow.

I have witnessed a team's culture change—for better and for worse—with the addition of a single team member. I have seen a positive, supportive culture get swept away and replaced with one that lacks trust, support, and any positive feedback. It happened faster than I would have imagined possible.

In the interest of protecting the identity of the leader who became the catalyst for the negative change, I will not mention specifically when or where this occurred. I was a leader on a team of technical leaders working with a senior leader who practiced many of the behaviors I have discussed in this book. He was collaborative and supportive. He served the team by championing our causes, representing our interests, and fighting for the things that would make us more effective. He communicated well and was sincere and honest. When he made mistakes, he admitted them and asked for help when appropriate. He modeled the behaviors that built a productive, supportive, positive culture. My peers and I developed great relationships under his leadership and example. Our team practiced extreme collaboration—we constantly pitched in to help one another. At no point, before or since, have I been a member of a group that was more clearly on the same page, pulling in the same direction.

But then our company acquired another organization, and another technology team was added. Eventually, our senior leader moved on to do different things, and my peers and I began reporting to a senior leader from the acquired company. Everything changed. Fast. The new leader's actions showed that he valued image and appearance over honesty, collaboration, and transparency. He routinely said and did things that were dishonest and detrimental to the team. He did not communicate with me and my peers much, and never deeply. All conversations were superficial and focused on how we needed to help make sure he did not have to answer difficult questions for his peers or the CEO.

As a result of the new senior leader's behaviors, our team's extreme collaboration dried up quickly. Our team members all went into self-protection mode almost overnight. We didn't know how to continue operating with trust and sincerity when the leader overwhelmed us with contrary requirements. One leader after another was disciplined for taking actions with which the senior leader disagreed. He made it clear we would either follow his lead or suffer the consequences. Within a year, our team had undergone a transformation. Many of us chose to leave the company or were let go. A single senior leader dismantled our team's great culture in less than a year. And he made it look easy.

The right culture can be a competitive advantage in business and a force multiplier for the team—as we had before the new leader arrived. When a team or company's culture is encouraging and supportive, the members can be more engaged and motivated to work with excellence. Where a group's culture encourages collaboration, team members are more likely to share knowledge and ideas openly, leading to more effective problem-solving. A culture that encourages creativity and risk-taking can foster a more innovative environment, allowing team members to experiment and make startling discoveries.

As a leader, you are in a good place if you find yourself planted in a company with a positive culture that encourages transparency and trust. Such a culture can act as a positive support structure as you focus on building your career ethically. Imagine how much easier it will be to establish trust in your team if the company's culture expects trustworthy actions and fosters trust among its members.

Imagine how much easier it will be to solicit candid feedback from your team members if the company's culture holds such feedback in high esteem. How much easier will it be to be honest and vulnerable with your team if the company's executive leadership models the way?

A company with the right culture can be the birthplace of the integrity edge. On the other hand, toxic culture is a stumbling block of external influence that can derail even the most dedicated ethical leader. Growing your career with integrity can be difficult. In any environment, countless challenges will represent opportunities for missteps. When you combine all the expected challenges with a culture that encourages shortcuts and compromises, the combination can be overwhelming.

**A company with the right culture
can be the birthplace of the integrity edge.**

Let's define toxic culture. The culture of a team or company embodies how things are done within the organization. It is the collection of values, beliefs, behaviors, and habits that define how the company operates and how its employees experience it. Culture is not just the things the company says are important; instead, culture is the result of the actions that employees and leaders of the company take and tolerate. It is a result of action and inaction, not words and sentiments. Toxic culture is when the actions and inactions of the company result in a culture that is detrimental to the employees. Toxic culture is characterized by negativity, fear, and dysfunction. Toxic culture is not cured by crafting a well-written company values statement. Flowery words and aspirational statements do not make up for the toxic actions of company employees and leaders.

Toxic culture presents in many different ways. A company can allow frequent criticism, blaming, and gossip, thereby creating a hostile environment. Some companies, through their actions and inactions, create a culture that tolerates bullying or harassment, which creates a toxic environment for employees. Some leaders use fear and intimidation to motivate employees, stifling creativity and innovation. A culture where employees don't trust each other or their leaders can hinder collaboration and productivity. Some leadership teams fail to hold employees accountable for their actions, resulting in a sense of injustice and resentment. In each case, the company's culture is born as a result of the actions taken by the team members—both leaders and individual contributors.

When the new senior leader arrived at our company, he brought with him the seeds of toxic culture. Everyone on his team was repeatedly presented with the toxic culture stumbling block from that day on. Every day, we each ran the risk of being negatively influenced by his brand of culture. Those who followed the senior leader's path were forced to make choices that did not align with our goals of leading with integrity.

When you find yourself working for a team with a toxic culture, you have three options. Fortunately, two of the three options allow you to avoid the toxic culture stumbling block completely.

First option: You can try to change the toxic culture by taking a stand and demonstrating the behaviors that will improve the culture. This is the difficult option.

Second option: You can leave the company. You may realize you are being negatively impacted more than you are making a positive influence, and leaving the company is the only way to preserve your integrity edge. This is the disappointing option, but it is an option that allows you to continue your mission of growing your career ethically.

Third option: You can change your actions to match the toxic culture. You can give in and abandon your desire to lead with integrity. You can accept the destructive patterns of the culture and get along. This is the path of the toxic culture stumbling block. This option leads to ethical compromise and failure of character.

Make no mistake—choosing the third option means abandoning your goal of ethical advancement. When you decide to adopt the toxic culture, you choose all of the compromise, selfish choices, and despicable decisions that go along with it. Accepting toxic actions and unethical or harmful decisions without resistance puts your character at risk. It is not possible to make this choice without being negatively impacted.

Since you have made it this far in a book entitled *The Integrity Edge*, I will take a leap and believe that you do not see compromising your character, using people, and generally acting like a selfish jerk as a viable option. C. S. Lewis famously wrote, "Integrity is doing the right thing, even when no one is watching." Integrity also demands that one does the right thing even when everyone around you is not doing the right thing. As such, we will focus on the only two options you have if you find yourself working in an environment with a toxic culture: change it or leave it.

CHAMPION FOR CULTURE CHANGE

I won't sugarcoat this: Trying to change toxic culture in any environment is a rough road. It is often a lonely road. There is no guarantee that you will actually be successful. Indeed, leaders who start down this path often decide (or are forced) to leave the environment long before their efforts to change the toxic culture bear lasting fruit. Choosing this path means you will pit yourself against "the way things are done" at the company. You set yourself up to be the person who "doesn't get along" with others at the company. Others may label you with any number of hateful titles. This is the price of the "change it" path. You must be willing to stand against "normal" and stand out as "different."

When you make this choice, you will be the Champion for Culture Change. Let's get you ready for the battle ahead. We need a plan. Let's discuss the behaviors you must adopt and some of the actions you will take in your pursuit. You will have to tweak these recommendations to your specific situation, but they can serve as the framework for your successful struggle.

Behaviors

As the Champion for Culture Change (that has a nice ring to it, doesn't it?), you have a mighty daunting hill to climb. The climb will probably be long, it will be lonely at times, and there is no certainty of success. You can lean into some specific behaviors to help you during this climb. These behaviors are not unique to being a Champion for Culture Change. They are helpful in general—anytime and for anyone who is committed to taking an unpopular path.

Be Courageous

You're probably thinking, "Really, Rusty? We are getting ready to stand against the system, potentially putting our jobs on the line, and your advice is to 'be courageous'? I think we already figured that out."

That's fair. Of course you realize that choosing to stand against toxic culture and be the Champion for Culture Change will require uncommon courage. But still, it bears talking about for a bit. You are going to have to speak boldly to people in positions of power. You are going to see things that epitomize the toxic culture, and in that moment, you are going to have to say something.

Imagine you are a director at a large company. The culture of this place is toxic to the core. Leaders at your company do not respect the employees of the company or their opinions. This place has a "be seen and not heard" attitude toward non-management employees. Female employees, in particular, are disrespected and dismissed as irrelevant.

Employees have learned their lessons. After witnessing senior leaders repeatedly put employees in their place, individual contributors within the company have been effectively cowed. The disrespect and public corrections and chastisement often even include supervisors and managers. Everyone at the company has learned that their opinions don't matter. If they want to keep their jobs, they just need to keep their mouths shut and do whatever they are told—even when the things they are told to do are nonsensical.

You have had enough. You have decided you cannot continue to work in a culture that completely disrespects its people. You are especially sick of the way female employees are treated at your company. You have decided to stand up to the toxic culture and do what you can to change it.

You are in a large conference room with a few of your team members, a few of your director peers, and your direct manager—the vice president. One of your team members, a female employee named Leah, has just finished presenting on a topic on which she is the company expert—nobody in the company knows the material as well as Leah. After her presentation, one of your peers comments that the conclusions Leah presented are incorrect and proceeds to introduce a new set of conclusions. When Leah attempts to offer a rebuttal in support of her conclusions—the conclusions she reached after weeks of research and hard work—she is told by the vice president, "Quiet, the adults are talking."

You decided to take a stand against the toxic culture, and there you sit, witnessing it firsthand. This situation calls for immediate and appropriate action. The appropriate action requires you to say or do something that lets the vice president and other directors know that you are not on board with the way they treat the team. Appropriate action cannot wait until you feel more comfortable or have a chance to prepare. You must speak up now, in the moment, if you have any hope of changing this culture.

Wow. Can you imagine? Well, get ready. This sort of scenario will unfold countless times in your struggle as the Champion for Culture Change. You will find yourself as the only voice against the toxic actions you witness. In time, you will gain allies, but initially, you will be one voice. Being a single, contrarian voice in the face of powerful opposition requires courage.

So, while it may be obvious, it bears some discussion. You must be courageous as the Champion for Culture Change.

We previously discussed courage in the chapter about the fear stumbling block (chapter 3). In that chapter, I suggested faith, purpose, and conviction as tools for creating courage. If we invest in developing these tools for a specific belief, idea, or principle, it can create weapons-grade courage that we can bring to bear in the conference room from our example.

There is no shortcut to investing in your courage-creating tools. Growing your faith, purpose, and conviction requires no great skill or talent. It only requires time and attention. If you focus on these things—what they mean to you, why they are important, and where you might end up without them—they will grow stronger in time. This approach is like a good running game in American football, or erosion—stick with it long enough, and it will produce results.

Take some time and think about why you are unwilling to "go along to get along" with the actions that are common in the toxic culture. Why does it matter? Standing against toxic actions will likely draw unwanted attention from those in power who engage in such behavior. Why are you willing to put yourself through that? Truly focus on your thoughts about this.

How does it make you feel to realize that each day, employees are disrespected as a matter of routine operations? How does it make you feel when you remember how the vice president talked down to your employee—an expert who had completed weeks of research to be the most informed person in the room—simply because she didn't have the right title or gender?

Consider how being around these actions influences your actions. Are you acting differently than you did when you first arrived at this company? Do you see any ways the toxic actions of your peers and boss are influencing what you see as acceptable and unacceptable?

Take time to focus on the impact that toxic culture and the hateful actions it creates have on you and your team members. Consider what will happen to them and you if nothing changes. Consider whether you can accomplish your goal of growing your career ethically if you are surrounded by coworkers, peers, and senior leaders who condone toxic actions.

Let your time of discovery on these topics help you strengthen your conviction to act. If you come to the conclusion I expect you will (i.e., you cannot tolerate these actions and be the person you want to be), the prospect of having to find another job will be less daunting. Your conviction and purpose will strengthen as courage-creating tools. You will be encouraged, realizing that standing against toxic culture is not only the right thing, but other than leaving the company, it is also the only choice that aligns with your goal of growing your career ethically. Moreover, you may come to realize that you are not all that upset over the idea of losing your job because you stood against the toxic culture of your company. After all, if nothing changes about the culture, you cannot accomplish your career goals at a company with a toxic culture.

So, back to the condescending, disrespectful vice president. Something has to be done, and it needs to be done while the perpetrators and the victim are still in the moment.

Consider the following in your response:

1. Champion your team member.
2. Remind the audience of the time she has spent researching this topic and her expertise in the subject matter.
3. Elaborate on her ideas and defend her ideas.
4. To the collected group, state that she is best positioned to provide expert advice on this topic.
5. Finally, remind them that even if we decide to go in a different direction, her work, expertise, and experience deserve gratitude.
6. It is likely best to do all of these things without calling out your vice president directly. Use your

actions to show your preferred approach rather than attacking the toxic culture head-on.

It might sound like this:

Calmly, directing your comments to the director who disagreed with Leah, you might say, "Hold on, Jerry. Leah has the data. She researched this down to the smallest detail. It's right there in her presentation and the pre-read she sent to all of us yesterday. If I recall correctly, her pre-read material had an entire section about your point, and even explained why it might not be the best approach. We are making a mistake if we do not acknowledge that she knows this data better than us. I cannot specifically speak to your opinion, but given that she has researched this topic more thoroughly than we have, I recommend we consider her response.

"Leah, can you provide your perspective on the points Jerry raised? What does your research say about his point of view?"

It will take courage to stand up like this, and it will not be the last time you have to do it. The more you do it, the easier it will be to do it again.

As I mentioned, strengthening these courage-creating tools does not require any specific skill or talent and does not necessitate following a complex procedure. Take time. Be honest. Look deep. And focus on what you discover.

Be Patient

Consider all the changes that must be made to transform your company's culture. Think about how long the current actions have been accepted and expected. Think about the company's employees who actively encourage the toxic culture. That's a lot, right?

Culture change takes time. Consider the Apple turn-around after Steve Jobs returned as CEO and the Microsoft turnaround after Satya Nadella was named CEO. In both cases the new CEO took over a company with a culture that was not congruent with the new CEO's desired direction. Neither company was necessarily toxic, but neither company had the culture their new CEO desired. In both cases, the new CEO ultimately succeeded in their culture turnaround efforts, but the efforts unfolded over many years. The change took years, even when the Champion for Culture Change was the new CEO. Perhaps you noticed that my former boss tore down our great culture in a year, but now I am telling you it will likely take many years to turn around toxic culture. This is the sad reality. You could say culture is like a tree. It takes years to grow but a short time to cut it down.

You can bet your mission to impact your company's culture positively is going to take time. There will be setbacks. There will be times when you think you are making no difference. There will be losses. Some days, you will wake up and wonder what you have gotten yourself into and question why you keep trying.

You will notice, as in the situation with Leah, we didn't immediately try to chastise the vice president for his actions. What would have been the point? We need to be willing to make small, incremental progress.

Be patient. Don't give up on your goals. Learn from each engagement. Don't try to change the culture with one epic action. We will discuss some actions you can take in the upcoming section. Spoiler: none of the recommendations is a big bang. Be willing to stack small—sometimes tiny—victories as you work. One engagement at a time. This approach takes patience.

Be Resilient

Resilience is the ability to face challenging situations, persevere, and be prepared for the next challenge. It is the ability to recover from adversity. It is the ability to adapt to challenging experiences and maintain positive psychological well-being in the face of stress.

Raise your hand if you would like some of that. Whether we are gearing up to face off against toxic culture or just preparing for next Monday, we might all appreciate being a little more resilient. As with many of the topics in this book, there is no Easy Button or magic wand to add additional resilience to your toolbox. However, there are strategies we can employ to help foster resilience and cultivate a resilient mindset.

Let's start with things you can do to help ensure you maintain a healthy mindset during the trying times. Running into obstacles and roadblocks day after day with few tangible victories to show for your pain and effort will take it out of you. You must have coping mechanisms that will help you weather the storm and stay resilient for the next day's challenges. There are experts in this field who can tell you about brain chemistry and advise you on your psyche. I recommend that you utilize those resources, as they can provide additional ways to cope. However, this book focuses on the methods I have personally employed as I have grown my career ethically. We will focus on two—stress management and cultivating a positive mindset.

Stress is a killer. Well, perhaps stress doesn't hold the gun, but stress is implicit in a myriad of adverse physical conditions. Stress can create anxiety and depression. Stress can impair cognitive functions and can negatively impact memory and decision-making. Stress sucks. Unfortunately, there is no quick fix for stress. More unfortunately, the things we need to do to help deal with stress may seem small and insufficient. I have noticed most folks are more willing to attempt a complex, expensive, or dangerous solution to a problem before they will do the small, simple, free things that must be done over and over. We would appreciate a one-time fix, even if it is expensive or dangerous, rather than having to discipline ourselves to do something small repeatedly.

The most effective ways to deal with stress are a collection of small, simple things that we must do over and over again. Don't shoot the messenger, especially since I am almost certain you already know this message. Exercise, sleep, time management, social support, and time disconnected from our stressors are some small, yet simple things we can do to help alleviate stress.

I have proof. Well, I think I have proof. I wear an advanced fitness tracker watch. I wear it all the time, other than when I am in the shower because it is charging. That means I wear it when I am working, when I am relaxing, when I am exercising, and when I am sleeping. It tracks heart rate. It tracks steps. It tracks sleep quality. All the things. Among its many great features, this watch tracks "stress."

This watch uses a few heart-related measurements as an analog for stress. The watch displays stress on a chart where short blue lines indicate low stress and tall orange and red lines indicate higher stress. Wearing this watch has made me hyperaware of the stress I am enduring. Without the watch, I could convince myself that I'm fine. But the watch knows. It knows when I haven't slept well. It knows when I get worked up in a business conversation. It even knows when I drink alcohol. I know that it knows because my stress chart correlates with my actions.

I have witnessed the impact of exercising three times a week has on my stress. I am not a professional athlete or gym rat—it's not that type of exercise. I exercise because I want to be healthy enough to enjoy my family for as long as I possibly can. I exercise because I am selfish and don't want to leave my loved ones prematurely. I can directly correlate reduced stress markers with exercise. When I exercise, my stress chart looks more blue. I have also noticed that when I don't exercise for a few days in a row, the positive impact on my stress markers diminishes, and orange returns to my stress chart. I witness this correlation every time. More than that, when I exercise I get more productive sleep. Without exercise, my overnight stress markers are elevated compared to when I exercise. The sleep scores I get when I exercise are universally higher than the sleep scores I get when I do not exercise. Again, the watch knows.

I mentioned earlier that my watch knows when I drink alcohol. I don't have to tell it. When I drink alcohol, my stress markers skyrocket. In fact, there is nothing in my life that has a more dramatic negative impact on my stress chart than alcohol consumption. If I drink, my stress chart gets more orange. The more I consume, the more orange the chart gets. Also, when I drink, my sleep score tanks. Every time I consume alcohol, my stress markers peak into the orange zone and do not recover into the blue until well into the night's sleep. Sometimes, it never fully reaches the blue zone. On these nights, my watch is gracious enough to inform me that the sleep was "non-restorative."

This is important because good, restorative sleep is one of the most commonly stated stress reducers. Most sources indicate that 7–9 hours of sleep is ideal, but I have learned that this is a highly personalized number. Each of us has a different ideal sleep duration, but we are all alike in one way. We must have sufficient restorative sleep if we are going to deal with our stress and remain resilient. I recommend you treat your sleep time as a productivity tool. Tell yourself—no, convince yourself—you cannot be successful in your career or as that Champion for Culture Change unless you are well-rested. Treat it like a critical success factor. It will not happen unless you prioritize it. That means prioritizing it over other things. Pro tip: couple intense exercise with good sleep habits. The exercise will wear you out and help you prepare for a restful sleep.

Time management, social support, and time spent being disconnected go hand-in-hand-in-hand. We cannot expect to work every waking hour while still managing our stress and being resilient. We must be able to disconnect and do things that recharge us.

I recommend you set office hours with yourself and your coworkers. Commit to complete focus on work tasks between set hours and on set days. Barring a true work emergency or a unique situation, stick to your office hours. It will take time to get your coworkers and yourself to respect these office hours, but it is time well spent. Introducing some predictability and structure into your day, including time away from work, is a key factor in reducing stress and building resilience. When we disconnect and engage in activities that bring us joy and happiness, we recharge. Time spent with loved ones and friends, time spent doing hobbies, time spent exercising, time spent doing nothing more than thinking, meditating, relaxing, or reading—these activities recharge the batteries you spent all day draining.

This time will not happen unless you prioritize it. Are you starting to see the pattern? Dealing with stress and cultivating resilience is primarily about prioritizing the things that fill you up. Left to our instincts, most humans will drain, drain, drain, and wonder why their tanks are empty and they are so stressed. We must also prioritize the things that fill us up, not just the things that drain us.

Actions

At this point, you are committed to changing the toxic culture you are witnessing. You have had enough, and you are willing to stand against the storm of toxic actions and consequences to be the Champion for Culture Change. You are embracing the behaviors that will support your challenge. You are investing in building your courage, patience, and resilience—knowing these behaviors will be crucial if you are to succeed. Let's discuss how you should approach changing the toxic culture that surrounds you.

It is likely obvious that your specific actions depend wholly on your situation. There is no way for us to script a perfectly detailed roadmap for your unique culture change initiative. There are far too many variables. The actions that work for me may doom you to failure. Instead, let's talk about a general strategy for how you can approach your battle to increase your odds of success. The general approach we will review is simple: start small, build a coalition, and seek help.

Start Small

The struggle to change toxic culture must start within your immediate sphere of influence. Specifically, the battle must begin with you and your actions. Take inventory of how you acted in the days and weeks before you decided to challenge your organization's toxic culture. You recognized the toxic culture and decided it could not continue—it had to change. Great.

Remember back to when you made that decision. Can you see things about your behavior at that time that suggest your coworkers' toxic culture and actions may have already influenced your actions? I suspect you can. You may have inadvertently mimicked an accepted practice that does not align with your core values. Perhaps it was nothing huge or overtly evil—a dismissive response to a subordinate or a passive-aggressive poke at an employee who logs off at 5 p.m. and doesn't check her email until the next day. Can you think of an action you would do differently if you had the chance to do it over again? Can you see something you did that aligns more with the toxic culture you hope to change than it does with your core values? That is where you start.

Commit to modeling the behaviors you wish to see in the company culture. Demonstrate the behaviors and attitudes you want to see in others. Your actions can be a powerful influence on others. Moreover, if you do not embody the change you champion, your crusade will appear disingenuous and contrived. If you are not an example of the change you champion, you risk being seen as part of the problem culture—out for personal gain and insincere. Your culture change must start with you.

If you are not an example of the change you champion, you risk being seen as part of the problem culture—out for personal gain and insincere.

Continue your efforts in your sphere of influence where you have authority. Your team should be the grass-roots start of the sweeping culture change you are pursuing. Institute the changes you want within your team first. Start by clearly stating the cultural characteristics you desire in your company. Don't make the mistake of pitting your team's culture against the organization's culture: "Our team will not be like the corporate executives. We will work together and treat one another with respect. We will not be back-stabbing jerks like the CEO is." Regardless of your good intentions, that sort of statement is likely the fastest possible path to derailing your fledgling resistance.

Instead, clearly and deliberately state the culture you desire. What are the characteristics you wish the company valued? Document them and hold them up as your team's values. How do you want your organization's employees to treat one another? Document those behaviors as the standard and only acceptable behavior for your team members. Write down the outcomes you are fighting for in clear, unambiguous terms. Having the outcomes clearly defined will allow you to bring others into the battle with you and allow you to craft your actions deliberately.

Earlier in my career, I served as the head of technology for a fast growing, post-startup company. It was not an accident that this company had a positive, uplifting culture and I was truly fortunate to work at an organization like it. Since the company was founded, their "High Five Values" were an integral part of their culture. Their "High Five Values" were:

1. Choose an optimistic point of view.
2. Have an innate curiosity.
3. Collaborate with brilliance and expertise.
4. Bring your best and expect the best from others.
5. Respect others and the value they bring.

These "High Five Values" were documented before I arrived at the company. Establishing values in this manner publicly articulates the type of culture you desire in your team or company. By declaring your values this way, you give voice to your cultural aspirations and provide a target for your team members.

Imagine you and I were planning a trip together—a vacation. We have been looking forward to our vacation. We have agreed on the dates of our time off, but we haven't discussed our destination. We each know the other is looking forward to the vacation and doing everything they need to do to prepare. I have been visualizing the rugged hikes across the Colorado Rocky Mountains and have prepared accordingly—backpack, hiking boots, bear whistle, all the essential things. Meanwhile, unbeknownst to me, you have been preparing for a beach vacation in Florida. You are ready to relax in the surf and have prepared accordingly—suntan lotion, swimsuit, and sandals.

Silly example, right? Hopefully it illustrates the point. When we fail to clearly articulate our values, we leave the building of our team's culture to chance. If this company hadn't highlighted "optimistic point of view" in their values, how would the team members know that the company not only wants employees to collaborate and respect one another, but they highly value doing so with optimism? Perhaps they would reach the same destination, but they would be leaving a lot to chance. By documenting that value, they make their intentions clear and can better influence the culture that eventually forms as a result.

You should take the same approach as you start challenging your company's toxic culture. Define the values you want your coworkers to share with you. Be specific. Use this specific list of values as your starting point.

Armed with a list of values and a clear understanding of the aspirational culture you desire for your team, you can start looping others into your mission. Schedule a team meeting and talk about the importance of shared values and culture in a work environment. Help the team members understand why it is essential to be deliberate with your actions if you want a specific outcome. Use the list of values you created to steer the discussion. Encourage specific actions from your team members.

After the initial team meeting, where you introduce the notion of shared team values and being deliberate about the actions you take to see those values manifest, make discussions about culture and the importance of right action a recurring theme in your team discussions and one-on-ones. Work to make these elements part of your team's standard operating activities.

Your team should know they will discuss culture, values, and individual actions when meeting with you. This repetition, underpinned by seeing you act in the manner you are asking of them, will convert some of your team members. Some are like you, eager to see a better culture at the company. These team members will see your example as a path to something better and follow your lead.

Start small. Start by examining your actions. Start by articulating the values you want to model. Now that you have established this small start, layer on additional supporters—loop in the team members in your sphere of management influence. This path will be slow, but it allows you the best chance to begin influencing your company's toxic culture.

Build a Coalition

Now that you have established a firm foundation for the struggle against your company's toxic culture, it is time to find other leaders who share your frustration with the status quo or see what you see and are equally disappointed. Since you started small and established a foothold of resistance in your team, you will likely start garnering the attention of some of these folks. They should see that your team operates differently. They will recognize the actions of your team members and rightly discern that it is not an accident. This is your time to build a network of allies—a coalition for culture change.

The goal of this phase is to create a coalition of fellow leaders and coworkers who share your desire to change your company's culture. You want to create a united front of people whose actions embody the change you are fighting for. You don't create this coalition by sending a company-wide email and asking who wants to put their job at risk by standing against the company's toxic culture machine. You create this coalition through relationship building and honest, frank discussion.

Keep your eyes and ears open for other leaders who recognize your team's positive actions. Schedule one-on-one discussions with those folks. Share the values you have declared and describe how you are talking about values, culture, and the importance of right actions with your team members. Explain how you are including these topics in your team meetings and one-on-ones. Share your values statement. Offer to continue meeting with them from time to time to talk about these important topics. Encourage them to share these things with their team members.

I will repeat my caution from earlier in this chapter. Refrain from condemning and chastising the current culture and the leaders who support it. You do not have the position or authority to survive a campaign like that. Instead, focus on the values you hold dear and the actions those values demand of you. Focus on the actions you will take—not on the actions you wish other leaders would stop taking.

Focus on the actions you will take—not on the actions you wish other leaders would stop taking.

This coalition-building phase might be the most peril-ous stage of the resistance. During this phase, you share your personally created values outside your immediate team. You will almost certainly share your values and plans with individuals not fully sympathetic to your mis-sion. Even if you are careful not to criticize the current culture, some powerful people will see your actions as dangerous and disruptive. You knew there would be risks when you started down this path. Stay focused on the pos-itive values and the positive actions. It is not foolproof; you could still face sanction, reprimand, and disciplinary action. However, when you have "positive values and pos-itive actions" as your foundation, the opposition will not have much honest ammunition to work with.

Seek Help

You started by checking your actions, detailing your desired end state, and getting your team on board. Then, you ex-panded your circle to include other like-minded leaders. By now, you are making a difference. It might be small, but I have no doubt you are changing the culture. However, if you want this culture change initiative to survive and impact the entire organization, you will need help. You need the help of not only the coalition members you are cultivating within your company, but also the help of resources beyond those in your company. You need to leverage the experience, ad-vice, and support of people who have gone down this path before you. Once again, your professional network can come to the rescue.

We previously discussed ways your professional net-work can be valuable in your journey as an ethical leader. I hope you have been investing time in developing your network by meeting new professionals within and outside of your industry. For many people, networking activities—social mixers, meet-and-greet type events, creating conversation with strangers—are off-putting. Many professionals despise these activities. I get it. I urge you to press through the discomfort and engage in professional networking. The dividends a solid network delivers are wide-reaching. Your network will be crucial in your struggle against your company's toxic culture.

As the Champion for Culture Change, you will find like-minded professionals in your network who have experience with toxic culture and positive culture. You will find people who have successfully navigated culture change, and some who failed to bring about the changes they sought. In every relationship, there are lessons to be learned. Find out how they successfully engaged with difficult individuals and situations. Ask them what strategies they found effective in their culture change experiences. Listen to their stories of success and failures, find commonalities with your reality, and glean what useful bits they offer that you might bring to bear in your journey.

When you discuss your journey with these positive culture warriors, you can find more than recommendations and advice. These discussions may provide emotional support and validation. When leaders feel isolated or unsupported in a toxic environment, having a network of peers can help them maintain their morale and sense of personal value. The connections can help you remember why you agreed to this struggle in the first place. Knowing you are not alone can be a powerful motivator, especially when you struggle to see any positive impact from your actions.

Beyond finding support from the people in your network, we need to leverage some specific types of contacts in our struggle. We previously discussed the value of finding mentors and coaches. Both mentors and coaches could be valuable allies as you navigate changing your company's toxic culture. However, mentors and coaches are not the same and may approach your request for assistance differently.

Mentorship typically involves a long-term relationship built on trust and mutual respect. A mentor may offer wisdom and advice based on their own experiences. Coaching, on the other hand, is typically a more structured and time-bound professional relationship. Coaches are often trained professionals with specialized knowledge in coaching methodologies and techniques. Mentors rely on their experience, while coaches rely on their training and processes. Both approaches deliver results, and it is often helpful to leverage both models simultaneously. As a Champion for Culture Change, you will benefit from both types of support.

When It Is Time to Go Big

At some point in your resistance, you will come head-to-head with a supervisor or direct manager who is part of the toxic establishment. This is where most of the danger in the resistance will be felt. How do you get your toxic boss to change? Or at least, how do you get your toxic boss to leave you alone as you work on positively influencing the company's culture?

A frontal assault on your toxic boss is precarious. There is likely never going to be a good time to tell him you think he is part of the problem and the cause for your company's toxic culture. Let's agree that we will use this as a last option on the day that you are prepared to tender your resignation.

A better plan for "going big" will be to find coalition members who are at your boss's level or higher. While they may be few and far between, there is a chance your company has a senior leader who shares your point of view and can be infected by your passion for change. Finding senior-level coalition members should be your "go big" goal. Let those coalition members engage with your boss and other senior team members as peers and subordinates. I think of this as bringing a gun to a gunfight. Like it or not, your authority might never provide you the firepower to enter that gunfight. You stick to the fights for which you have the right weapons (authority) to compete. Leave the gunfights to your senior coalition members.

Be courageous, be patient, and be resilient. Start small, build a coalition, and seek outside help. There is no guarantee you will be successful in your quest to change your company's toxic culture, but it is a worthy challenge. Standing up to powerful, influential people in positions of authority who are doing "bad things" is an almost noble pursuit, and it is the best kind of servant leadership. The return on efforts will be felt even if full victory is not achieved. Along the way, the small victories you and your team experience will be surprisingly fulfilling. Godspeed, Champion for Culture Change!

IF YOU CAN'T BEAT 'EM . . .

When you determine you will not be able to change the toxic culture you are experiencing, you are left with being influenced by it or leaving it. Allowing yourself to become the thing that toxic cultures produce is unacceptable. You would not be reading this book if you thought becoming a toxic leader was a viable path for your career. This is a case of "if you can't beat 'em, leave 'em" because "joining 'em" is simply not an option.

Leaving for another role is an appropriate response if you cannot make progress. Do not stay so long that the unethical, self-service model becomes normal to you. Do not stay so long that you are desensitized. At that point, toxic culture starts looking normal. You cannot allow that to happen. However, you also don't want to rush into leaving. You need to prepare.

Develop a strategy for your departure. Start a stealthy job search. You will want to keep the fact that you are looking for a new role secret as long as possible. Selfish, self-absorbed leaders seeped in toxic company culture are not known for respecting individuals' right to choice. Things will be more challenging when they discover you are looking for a new role. Engage with your network and recruiters, but ensure anyone you engage with understands the need for extreme confidentiality.

Consider any non-compete agreements you may have signed when you started this job. Are there companies or industries you should avoid in your job search? If you are in a niche field, consider engaging a lawyer to explore legal avenues to alleviate non-compete challenges.

The job market can be a fickle beast. The unpredictable nature of the job market is why I cannot confidently recommend that you leave your current role without a new role. There is no telling how long it will take you to find a new position. Sometimes these things happen so fast it will surprise you. Other times, excellent, high-performing candidates can be unemployed or underemployed for months—even years.

As you work through your job search, focus on companies with great cultures rather than roles with great titles. Ideally, you will land a role with a great title and compensation at a company with a great culture, but if you have to choose, choose culture. Again, use your network to research your target companies. When you get an interview with a new company, find out who you know at that company or who you know that knows someone there. Schedule an informal "information interview" with that person and ask them about the company. Your goal in these interviews is not to attempt to cultivate a reference at the company, but to learn everything you can about what it is like to work there. Ask questions that shed light on the areas where your current company is lacking—are leaders respectful, is the environment collaborative, how are employees empowered to do their best?

Expand the range of roles you are willing to accept during your search. Refrain from only looking at roles equal to or more senior than your current role. Examine your financial situation, bank account balances, and expenses. How long can your finances tolerate accepting a smaller salary or being without a job at all? If you have the flexibility, consider taking a slightly junior role from what you are accustomed to. It can provide a springboard effect in your new role. Take the junior role, outperform all expectations, and parlay that performance into a rapid promotion. This is a tried-and-true path and might help you find a new role faster.

How to Leave Well

Many years ago, I was impacted by a layoff. I had been serving as a director for a telecommunications company. When I was laid off, I was fortunate to receive some severance that would hopefully allow me to find a new role without too much financial burden. I decided to focus my search not only on director roles, but also on manager and individual contributor roles. I quickly got a job as a contractor in an individual contributor capacity. I worked in that contractor position for fewer than three months when the company I contracted for offered me a manager role. I accepted the manager role. Fewer than four months later, I was offered a promotion to a director role where I worked for more than four years. This example illustrates two things clearly—you can use roles for which you are overqualified as a springboard for a promotion, and opportunity plays a tremendous role in promotion. We cannot know if this sort of perfect storm of opportunity will happen at your new company, but we can be sure of your ability to deliver stand-out performance in a role that is junior to what you have been doing. Do not be afraid to take a chance. Being a manager for a company with a positive, uplifting culture is far superior to being a director at a company with a toxic culture.

Once you find your new role, you should do everything you can to exit well. Provide ample notice to your supervisor. Notify your supervisor of your decision to leave, providing a clear and concise explanation—not hateful or vindictive, but clear and concise. Be professional. Maintain a professional demeanor throughout the process, even when the situation becomes difficult. If you are offered an exit interview, participate in the process and provide honest feedback about your experience at the company and the role the company's toxic culture played in your decision. Come to the exit interview prepared to provide specific examples of the actions and behaviors that make the culture toxic. Your efforts may not make a difference, but they might be the seed of change. You could be planting the seed of positive culture change as you leave, and all it will cost you is some preparation time and a very uncomfortable conversation. That sounds like a good deal to me.

If you are not asked to participate in an exit interview, consider asking your human resources partner for one. Toxic cultures are often unwilling to accept any critique of their toxic ways, but what do you have to lose? It would be an uncomfortable discussion since they didn't recommend the interview on the tiny chance your feedback can be a seed for change, but I recommend you endure the discomfort and respectfully and professionally share your thoughts. Under no circumstances should you, in this last mile, resort to their toxic behaviors.

As you move on from your role, my most important recommendation is to maintain your integrity through the process. It could get ugly. Those in authority at companies with toxic cultures are not known for being kind, introspective, servant leaders. It is unlikely they will thank you for your feedback. They will not thank you for shedding light on their toxic actions and wish you well. More likely, they will get resentful and mean-spirited. Do not be drawn in. Stay on the high ground, integrity intact, and exit well.

SUMMARY

Toxic culture is driven by fear, negativity, and dysfunction. It stems from actions and inactions, not mission statements or values on paper. Leaders who tolerate harmful behavior perpetuate toxicity. When you find yourself in a company with toxic culture, you have three options:

1. Change it
2. Leave it
3. Accept it

Accepting it will not allow you to grow your leadership career with integrity. Changing it and leaving it are your only viable options. If you choose to stay and fight, know this:

- Change requires courage. Build up your courage by gaining and sharing a deep understanding of your mission, the team mission, and the company mission.
- Be patient.
- Be resilient.
- Build a coalition of change agents.
- Seek help from people outside the company who have stood against toxic culture in the past.
- Pick the right time to go big.

If you are forced to leave, leave properly. Plan your exit, find a new role before you exit if you can, and do not allow yourself to get pulled down into the toxic mud.

FIVE WHYS

What Drives Me Personally
& How You Can Discover What Drives You

*"The two most important days in your life are the day
you are born and the day you find out why."*

—MARK TWAIN

THROUGHOUT THIS BOOK, we have discussed the six stumbling blocks to ethical advancement, and I hope we have provided you with some strategies and defenses against them. If you stay aware of the risks the stumbling blocks represent and resist becoming a self-absorbed leader, you can seize the integrity edge. You can grow in your career as a leader without sacrificing your character or acting contrary to your integrity.

As we wrap up this book, I have just one final recommendation. I saved this one for last because, in many ways, this is the most important strategy of all. It is the umbrella under which you will perform all the other activities discussed in this book. It is the foundation from which all the strategies we discussed are born.

GETTING TO WHY

Why do you refuse to sacrifice your character and integrity as you grow your career? Look around—there are many examples of leaders who have reached lofty heights by focusing on themselves and not being burdened with how their ascension negatively impacts the people in their charge. It is a well-trodden path that you could follow—likely with less personal cost than the path you have chosen. Why are you choosing what might be the more challenging way?

My final recommendation is that you spend whatever time it takes to articulate the answer to that question. Why are you choosing the more challenging path?

Having a solid understanding of your personal motivation can act as an anchor during difficult and trying times. When the stumbling blocks start clouding your judgment, but you feel compelled to make a decision, leaders who best understand their motivation can lean on that anchor for clarity. It acts as a more stable foundation for decision-making and can help you make decisions that align with your core values.

Preparing a greeting-card-style definition of what motivates you will not be enough. If you have a superficial understanding of your motivation, it will offer superficial anchoring to your core values. When the forces of the stumbling blocks stack up, it will take more than a superficial understanding of why you choose to be a leader with integrity to overcome them.

Also, it won't be enough if you attempt to stand on an aspirational motivation. What is an "aspirational motivation"?

Aspirational motivation is shallow motivation based on what you wish you were passionate about rather than something you are actually passionate about. This sort of motivation lacks deep grounding and is seldom sufficient to influence behaviors over the long run.

Let's use a classic example of *aspirational motivation*—"I go to the gym because I want to be healthy." There are some folks who are truly motivated by being healthy. These folks eat the right food and avoid the wrong food. They stay active and mix in periods of more intense exercise. People who are actually motivated to be healthy have a relationship with a healthcare professional—or team of professionals—who ensure they know how healthy they are.

These people are not just motivated in the New Year's resolution season; they are also motivated in the dog days of summer. They are motivated when it rains. They are motivated when it is too hot, and they are motivated when it is too cold. They are motivated when they sit down to their favorite meal and are asked if they would like seconds—or thirds. In every situation, people who are deeply motivated to be healthy count the costs of violating that motivation.

On the other hand, someone driven by *aspirational motivation* wishes they were the kind of person who works out in the rain and stops eating after just one serving of their favorite indulgent meal. But when the decision is "let's be healthy" or "let's eat a second piece of pie," those who only possess aspirational motivation choose the pie.

Aspirational motivation is a fine place to start, but there must be more depth to the motivation if it is going to serve as your anchor and backstop. As the aspirationally motivated person sits in the house on a rainy afternoon instead of hitting the road to jog, you will also sit idle, as avoiding the stumbling blocks becomes too difficult. You'll need more than positive aspirations to make it through this journey.

Is your motivation to value character over career advancement true motivation or aspirational motivation? You need to dig deep and be honest with yourself. If you want to dig deep, try the "Five Whys" technique to help you uncover your deeper motivations. It's not a magic technique, but it might be helpful.

FIVE WHYS

I have led technical operations teams for nearly thirty years. One thing all technical operations teams have in common is that, from time to time, they deal with technology that doesn't work the way it was designed to. Every technical operations team occasionally has to troubleshoot a technical issue in the middle of the night or early on a Saturday morning. When the company's systems break, someone has to fix them. The systems rarely schedule the outages to be convenient for the technical operations team.

When there is a system outage, the most important thing the team has to do is correct the outage and recover the system. There is nothing more important. However, once the system is up and running, the most important thing the team needs to do is determine why it happened. We call the reason for the outage the "root cause." After the system is running again, nothing is more important than understanding the root cause of the outage and what can be done to eliminate that cause from creating future outages.

One technique we use to identify root causes is often called the "Five Whys." It is a shockingly simple technique. Essentially, it requires you to ask "why?" five times. Clever name, right?

I get the technical operations team together and ask, "Why did the outage occur?" Once the discussion arrives at an answer, I ask, "Why did that happen?" And then, "Why did that lead to this outcome?" Then, "Why did that result in this?" And finally, the fifth question: "Why did that cause this problem?" By asking "why" five times, you get past the superficial and dig deeper to find the actual root.

We can use a similar technique to uncover our deeper motivations. Start by blocking out some time on your calendar for introspection. Don't try to do this if you are distracted. Get alone and get focused. Power up your note-taking app—or pen and paper if you prefer old school tools—and start writing.

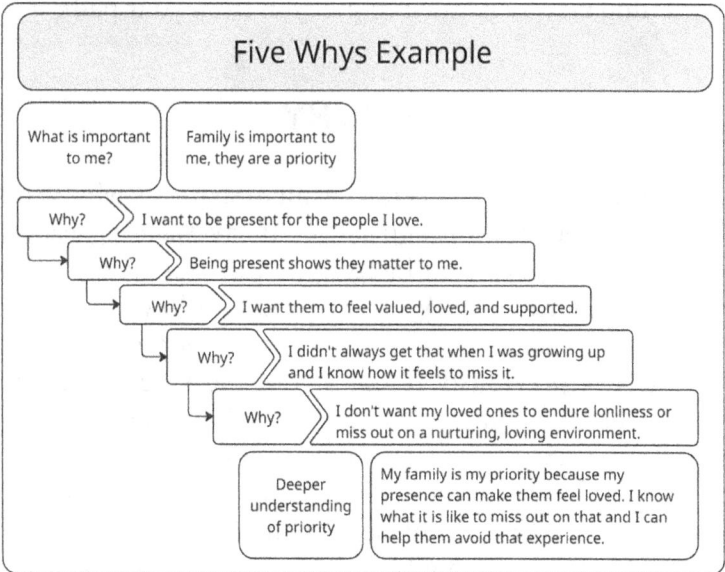

Five Whys Example

What is important to me?	Family is important to me, they are a priority

Why? ⟩ I want to be present for the people I love.

Why? ⟩ Being present shows they matter to me.

Why? ⟩ I want them to feel valued, loved, and supported.

Why? ⟩ I didn't always get that when I was growing up and I know how it feels to miss it.

Why? ⟩ I don't want my loved ones to endure lonliness or miss out on a nurturing, loving environment.

Deeper understanding of priority	My family is my priority because my presence can make them feel loved. I know what it is like to miss out on that and I can help them avoid that experience.

Why do you want to place a higher value on integrity than career advancement and refuse to compromise as you grow your career?

Why is this important to you?

Why do you place value on that?

Why is that important to you?

Why?

It is simple and effective for digging deeper. The answer to the first "why" will be superficial. Maybe the second "why" will be basic as well. But if you keep asking why, you force yourself to dig deeper into the root of your motivation. Writing down your thoughts as you work through this exercise is essential. Your goal is to get a deeper understanding of your motivation. Primarily, you want to be able to articulate your motivation to yourself. You want to get to the core of what makes you confident of your commitment to advance your leadership career ethically. You need the details to provide you strength and confidence when the stumbling blocks threaten to pull you from your path.

MY WHY

As this book comes to an end, I want to share my why. What has motivated me through nearly thirty years of leading people by character and integrity? I will present my motivation using the "Five Whys" method to help you visualize how it might help you better understand your motivation.

I did not previously reveal any of these details in this book. That was intentional and, candidly, more difficult than I expected. I hope I presented a logical, clear approach to growing your career in leadership without sacrificing your integrity. I hope I presented an entire toolbox full of things you can do to avoid the stumbling blocks that have tripped up so many leaders before you. I presented these tools on the merit of their efficacy. Regardless of what you discover as your "why," the tools defined in this book will be impactful. They will work for you if you use them.

OK, here's the big reveal: I am a Christian, motivated by my beliefs to act according to the Word and teachings of God.

Whether you share my beliefs or not, the principles I shared in this book are universal. I presented them as I did to encourage you to see that growing your career as an ethical leader with integrity is possible for anyone, not *only* if you are a Christian. It is possible for anyone who makes ethical decisions and refuses to compromise.

I presented the material in a secular format to encourage you to believe that the integrity edge is available to everyone who will prioritize treating people the right way. The only prerequisite for this approach to be successful is that you stick with it and never allow your motivation for career advancement to outstrip your motivation to treat people the right way.

The following are my five whys:

1. ***Why?***

   I want to retain my character and convictions as I grow my career because I see how some other leaders use their teams for personal gain, which never seemed right. I didn't want to do the same. I want to succeed in my leadership career, but I do not want to lose sight of the harm some actions have on the people I am responsible for leading. I never want to get to a place where getting promoted and being a successful leader comes at the expense of the people I am responsible for leading.

2. ***Why is that important to you?***

   I am a Christian man. My relationship with God is a priority to me and my family. I take that relationship seriously. I believe the way many leaders treat their people is unacceptable in the eyes of God. It seems to me that since, in most situations, a leader in the corporate, secular world cannot openly share God's message, many self-professed Christians simply stop acting according to God's

Word at work. Some seem to believe there are two gods. The God they openly worship in church, and the God that they actively ignore and silence in the workplace.

The fact is, there is one God. The God of the sanctuary is the God of the boardroom. He is the same God. His way is the same in both settings. His expectations are the same in both settings. My responsibility as His follower is the same in both places. Serving God in my place of work is the least I can do if I believe in God. I must treat the people I work with differently than the example I have seen so often from some leaders. In fact, when I do not treat people the right way, I am denying God in my life, and that is unacceptable.

3. *Why is it so important that you do things God's way?*
Early in my career, I recognized that I have strengths in areas I cannot explain. I hadn't gotten any training in these areas. I looked at my family and didn't see these strengths as common family traits. I looked at my parents and didn't see these strengths. And yet, I recognized these strengths early in my career. These gifts have been instrumental in my success as a leader.

I believe these strengths are God-given. If that is correct, and the gifts are given by God—why did He give them to me? What am I supposed to do with the gifts?

Many years ago, I believed God was preparing me for a life working in the church as a teacher or a pastor. I was unsure of what role I would serve, but I believed I would eventually leave the corporate world and work full-time in a church setting.

As I pressed into understanding what He was calling me to do, however, I realized He was calling me to a secular career. He gave me a gift and placed me in a corporate setting, and that is where He wanted me to thrive. He wasn't calling me to be another corporate leader who grows his career at the expense of those around him. But he was calling me to be a different kind of leader. He called me to stand out as an example of how His way works in the corporate world (Matthew 5:14-16). I want to lead people with character because it is what God has called me to do, and it is what God has enabled me to do.

4. *Why is it important to you to do the work God has called you to do?*

I believe if I honor God in my work life, God will reward me. He will give me the ability to prosper in all aspects of my life. God is a rewarder of those who diligently seek Him (Hebrews 11:6). The Bible states that God gives us the ability to create wealth or the ability to prosper (Deuteronomy 8:18). I want to lead people in God's way because, when I do, He causes me to be successful—not just as a successful leader, but to prosper in all areas of my life.

5. *Why are you so confident when so many successful leaders have chosen a different path?*

Because if I lose this job, God is still my provider. When I honor Him in my actions, I confirm that He is my God. He will never leave me. He will never forsake me. If this job goes away, I am convinced He will lead me to the next one.

I am convinced my refusal to sacrifice my integrity has caused me to lose a job in the past. The culture at the company where I worked had changed, as I discussed in the chapter about toxic culture. The new boss routinely did things that did not align with my values and were not congruent with leading with integrity. I refused to change. I quickly moved from the "high potential, high performing" category to "we need to go in another direction." My performance hadn't changed, but the expectations and approach of the team had.

But, as I knew He would, God honored my commitment and actions. Before my severance ran out, I landed a new role where I flourished. I could treat people the right way without concern for the impact it might have on my career growth because God's got my back.

Take whatever time it requires to understand your "why" deeply. It will encourage you, motivate you, and sustain you. You will find your "why" helps you navigate every single stumbling block. You will find no greater weapon.

CONCLUSION

The Competitive Advantage of Leading the Right Way

THROUGHOUT THIS JOURNEY, we've examined the stumbling blocks that often derail leaders: lack of trust, pride, fear, ambition, disconnect, and toxic cultures. These obstacles can tempt even well-intentioned leaders into compromising their integrity. We've also explored the powerful truth that avoiding these stumbling blocks is not only possible, but the foundation of a fulfilling and successful leadership journey.

Avoiding these stumbling blocks allows you to grow your career without sacrificing your character. It ensures that your climb up the career ladder is not built on manipulation, self-interest, or fear, but on trust, authenticity, and service. This approach establishes you as a leader whose success is both ethical and sustainable.

However, in addition to providing strategies that help you advance your career with integrity, the leadership style described in this book will become your not-so-secret weapon. It will eventually define you and become evidence of your enduring character and an illustration of your priorities. It will become your leadership superpower.

Several years ago, I was responsible for technology, security, and product management at a healthcare company. Within the first year of arriving at the company, we made some enormous bets on the company's future in the investments we made in technology and product management. A key system the company had been using since they were founded was effective, but it was neither efficient nor flexible enough to support the vision we had for our growth. We knew we needed to replace the system but found no acceptable replacement in the market. We would have to build the system our company needed if we were going to see our vision realized.

Armed with a clear vision and the confidence of the executive team, we built a replacement system from scratch. It was well received and has positioned the company to achieve many of the goals that were not attainable with the previous system. The project was a resounding success. But I get ahead of myself—first, we needed to assemble a team to make our plan a reality.

I decided to ask a high-performing operations leader with no product management experience to take on the senior product management role. The employee was a long-tenured employee, having started with the company when it was founded. This leader grew her career through the ranks, performing nearly all of the customer-facing management roles before joining the corporate operations team. At every stop along the way, she was a runaway success. I had tremendous confidence in her domain knowledge. No one at the company knew more about the incumbent system or company operations than she did. I was equally confident in her potential and personal drive—I had seen it modeled over and over again. However, I recognized the risk of asking an operations leader with no experience in technology or product management to step into the head of product management at such a pivotal time. It was going to be a big lift for her.

She accepted the challenge and moved into the fledgling product management team. What followed was a year of firsts at our company. Over the following year, the team we assembled reimagined every aspect of the technical underpinnings that supported our company's service delivery efforts. We set up new policies, new processes, and new infrastructure. We introduced new planning, design, and development approaches. We assembled a team of developers, testers, and product owners. We developed a feedback system that allowed us to better understand what our users and leaders liked and disliked about the old system we were replacing and the new system we were building. Oh, and we developed a completely custom system from scratch.

The project was an overwhelming success. We delivered the new application on schedule and on budget. It received overwhelmingly positive reviews from our users and leaders. The migration to the new system went off without a hitch—literally, no hitches. The users marveled at how easy it was to use and how much better the workflow was than the previous system. It was a home run.

At the end of the year, I had the honor of delivering my new product leader's performance review. Obviously, it was a glowing evaluation. She had exceeded my expectations. We knew she would be successful, but we honestly expected more challenges. I am not suggesting we completed the project without any mistakes or setbacks. Of course, we had many challenges. But through it all, she kept pressing. She met each setback with a "How do we make this right and keep on schedule?" mindset. She never seemed daunted by the pressure or the importance of the situation. She just kept pressing.

Formally documenting my opinion of her work and delivering her performance review was a joy. I made sure she knew how proud of her I was and how grateful I was for her.

She was overwhelmed by the review. Obviously she knew she had done great work, but I don't think she was prepared to hear my opinion of its impact. She thanked me for the kind words and said, "I was only able to do what I did because I know you had my back. I would not have even taken the role if I didn't know you would support me in every way possible. Whenever I brought a problem or a setback to you, you would say, 'Let's figure out what we are going to do about this.' You went straight to how you could support me rather than dwelling on the failure or finding out who to blame. That empowered me. I knew I could take chances and you would support me. If I didn't have that support, there is no way we would have gotten the project completed in time."

Leading with integrity is not just a moral ideal but a profound advantage. Trust is the currency of leadership, and employees who trust their leaders are far more engaged, productive, and innovative. When employees feel safe sharing their ideas, taking risks, and making mistakes, their potential is unlocked. This is the integrity edge: a work environment where people thrive, enabling extraordinary results for the leader, the team, and the organization.

This is the integrity edge: a work environment where people thrive, enabling extraordinary results for the leader, the team, and the organization.

We have reviewed specific steps leaders can take to avoid stumbling as they grow their career in leadership. You likely noticed many of the steps to address individual stumbling blocks have merit across multiple stumbling blocks.

- Building and protecting trust supports authenticity, accountability, and humility.
- Practicing servant leadership combats pride and ambition, while fostering engagement and collaboration.
- Staying committed to honesty and transparency strengthens your team culture and creates a foundation for long-term success.
- Modeling the behaviors you desire from your team members and demonstrating your willingness to work alongside them in challenging situations builds trust, supports humility, encourages a healthy culture, and maintains effective connections with your team members.

These shared actions are a great place to start. By incorporating them into your daily leadership practice, you'll begin to see how integrity amplifies your influence and your team's impact.

However, before all these strategies, there is a foundational recommendation: **commit to ethical leadership early**. Decide to take an ethical approach to leadership as soon as possible. Today would be a good day to make that commitment. Making this commitment early will make it easier to stay on course as the stakes get higher. Establishing this matter in your heart and mind will help you summon the courage and discipline necessary to avoid the stumbling blocks to ethical advancement.

Leadership is a long game. While the road to advancement with integrity may sometimes be lonely and scary, it leads to meaningful, enduring, and deeply rewarding success. The strategies outlined in this book—building trust, embracing humility, modeling accountability, serving your team members, fostering authenticity, and cultivating a positive culture—are not quick fixes. They are commitments that will shape the kind of leader you become and the legacy you leave. This leadership style empowers others to achieve greatness and positions you as a leader who inspires lasting change—the integrity edge.

The journey begins with a decision. Commit to leading with integrity now. Start with the shared actions we've explored, and let your leadership be defined by trust, accountability, and service.

NOTES

i. Martin Luther King Jr., "Remaining Awake Through a Great Revolution," Commencement address at Oberlin College, Oberlin, OH, June 1965.

ii. Ralph Waldo Emerson, "Social Aims," in *Lectures and Biographical Sketches* (Boston: Houghton Mifflin, 1883), 113.

iii. Larry Senn and Jim Hart, *21st Century Leadership: Dialogues with 100 Top Leaders* (Rancho Santa Margarita, CA: Leadership Press, 1994).

iv. Warren Bennis, *On Becoming a Leader* (New York: Basic Books, 1989), 140.

v. Helmuth von Moltke the Elder, paraphrased from his military writings, as cited in Daniel Hughes, *Moltke on the Art of War: Selected Writings* (Novato, CA: Presidio Press, 1993), 92.

vi. Mike Tyson, interview with Bert Sugar, 1987.

vii. Jocko Willink and Leif Babin, *Extreme Ownership: How U.S. Navy SEALs Lead and Win* (New York: St. Martin's Press, 2015).

viii. John C. Maxwell, *The 17 Indisputable Laws of Teamwork: Embrace Them and Empower Your Team* (Nashville: Thomas Nelson, 2001).

ix. Simon Sinek, Start with *Why: How Great Leaders Inspire Everyone to Take Action* (New York: Portfolio, 2009).

x. Jack Welch and Suzy Welch, *Winning* (New York: Harper Business, 2005).

xi. Mohammad F. Anwar et al., *Love as a Business Strategy: Resilience, Belonging & Success* (Vancouver: Page Two Books, 2021), 27.

xii. Ibid., 31.

xiii. Ibid., 36.

xiv. Ibid., 45.

xv. Andy Stanley, *The Next Generation Leader: 5 Essentials for Those Who Will Shape the Future* (Sisters, OR: Multnomah Publishers, 2003), 44.

xvi. Jon R. Katzenbach, T*he Wisdom of Teams: Creating the High-Performance Organization* (Boston: Harvard Business Review Press, 1993), 229.